TWO BROTHERS IN THE FRENCH REVOLUTION

J.B. ROBERT LINDET

Député de l'ass. Législative, Convention.
Ministre des Finances.

† 1825.

Paris, VIGNERES, Ed! 3o, Quai de l'Ecole.

Drouart imp. r. du Fouarre.11. Paris.

TWO BROTHERS
IN THE
FRENCH REVOLUTION

Robert and Thomas Lindet

by

HUNTLEY DUPRE

ARCHON BOOKS
1967

Library of Congress Catalog Card Number: 67–19458
Printed in the United States of America

To my sons
Vladimir and John

Contents

Preface

BROTHERS ACTIVE IN THE FRENCH REVOLUTION were rare. Two who had significant though unspectacular, undramatic roles, were Robert and Thomas Lindet, provincials from Normandy of modest bourgeois background.

Thomas, the older, was a humane and reforming priest who became a member of two revolutionary assemblies, the National Assembly and the Convention, and represented the Department of the Eure in the Council of Elders during the period of the Directory. He was also constitutional, juring bishop of the Eure until he resigned and left the Church.

Robert Lindet, the major subject of this study, was a lawyer who, after holding municipal and departmental offices, became a member of the Legislative Assembly and of the Convention. As a member of the Committee of Public Safety during the crisis of the Revolution, he was responsible for the feeding and provisioning of the revolutionary armies and of France. He was a practical rather than a theoretical, philosophical revolutionary. Nonetheless, he was a thoroughly committed revolutionary. He had decided administrative talents and an amazing capacity for work—a bureaucrat *par excellence* in the best sense of the term. Both brothers were staunch and faithful republicans to the end of their long lives in 1823 and 1825.

These two revolutionaries have been neglected in twentieth-century scholarship. Amand Montier wrote an excellent biography, *Robert Lindet: Notice Biographique* (1899), using the family papers. In the same year he published the *Correspondance de Thomas Lindet (1789–1792)*. My own research on Robert Lindet was undertaken in 1950 in France, prompted by my earlier study

ix

of Lazare Carnot. Academic administration interrupted this new research for a decade. When I took it up again in 1961 I included Thomas Lindet. It seemed that his career opened a relatively neglected door to an understanding of many sincere reforming priests of the Revolution.

Modest and inconspicuous as the two brothers were when contrasted to the better known figures of the Revolution, they do illuminate it through their words and deeds, as representative of the conscientious and committed Republicans who comprised a substantial portion of the Revolutionary Assemblies.

I have not attempted a history of the Revolution and have assumed a considerable knowledge of the period on the part of the reader. I have sought, however, to provide enough of the narrative and the setting to give relevancy to the actions of the two brothers, and to fit them into the revolutionary epoch in a meaningful and living fashion. In general, I have preferred to let the record speak for itself rather than to introduce a particular interpretation. Since they represent many other unsung participants it seemed that this was a desirable means of revealing the thoughts and feelings of these two heirs of the Enlightenment, become actors in their own revolutionary times.

I am indebted to the American Council of Learned Societies for a substantial grant to assist me in my final research in France in 1961. I acknowledge gratefully the valuable and gracious courtesies of the librarians and archivists of the British Museum, the Archives Nationales, the Bibliothèque Nationale, the Archives Départmentales de l'Eure at Evreux, and the Bibliothèque Municipale of Bernay. I am grateful to Macalester College, to President Harvey M. Rice, and to the Committee on Sabbatical Leaves for the opportunity to return to France, and to the Committee on Research for a generous grant for research abroad, and a later grant for typing the manuscript. I am appreciative, too, of the interest in this work of my new colleagues in the College of St. Catherine where I am now teaching in retirement.

I have profited by the critical reading of a part of the manuscript and by the helpful comments of my son, Professor Vladimir A. Dupre. I am grateful to Professor Philip D. Jordan for his friendly and steady encouragement and counsel.

Finally, I owe a great deal to the interest, enthusiasm, inspiration and patience of my wife, both in the research abroad and in the writing and re-writing of the manuscript. I am warmly grateful to Joanne Du Charme for her competent and interested typing of most of the first draft and I am deeply indebted to Jean Wetterlin Watson not only for her professional skill in typing the intermediate and final drafts of the manuscript but also for her friendly and genuine interest in the study that was unfolding.

HUNTLEY DUPRE

Saint Paul
Minnesota
December, 1966

TWO BROTHERS IN THE FRENCH REVOLUTION

CHAPTER ONE

A Norman Priest and Lawyer on the Eve of the Revolution

THE FRENCH REVOLUTION was in the making for three or four generations before it broke out in 1789. This does not imply that the Revolution was inevitable. It means that its development can be traced from events occurring and conditions existing many decades before 1789. Finally, after the failure of reforms from the top, the only outcome of irreconcilable interests was revolution. In these preliminary generations great numbers of persons, known and unknown, contributed, wittingly and unwittingly, to its development.

The French Revolution, once begun, was made by dramatic, strong, controversial men such as Mirabeau, Danton, Marat, Desmoulins, Robespierre and Saint-Just. It was also made by less colorful persons such as Siéyès, Roland, Brissot, Vergniaud, Buzot, Barère, Carnot, Prieur de la Côte-d'Or, and Robert Lindet. It was made, as well, by hundreds and thousands of lesser men in Paris and in the provinces who were active in the revolutionary assemblies, in the Jacobin Clubs, in the communes, in the departmental and municipal administrations, and in the crowds. The Revolution was opposed by the counter-revolution of *émigrés*, defecting generals and by royalists from all classes. It was violently challenged by the royalist and Catholic Civil War in the Vendée.

The great convulsion gave historic careers to the decisive men in the telescoped and turbulent decade of revolutionary change. Without the Revolution they would have remained anonymous and unknown. It picked up men who were without opportunity in the Old Regime and offered them extraordinary chances for leadership and power. In the crisis of the Revolution in 1793–94 some of these politically inexperienced men improvised splendidly to defend France and the Revolution against her internal and external enemies. The Revolution shook up everyone. No one could be indifferent to the cataclysm. Men had to stand up and be counted. It was a moment of passion and of faith, either in the old or in the new.

Great numbers were ready for the Revolution, consciously or unconsciously. The times were out of joint, ripe for change. Men, particularly the bourgeoisie, were chafing under the political, social and economic inequities and disparities of the rigid Old Regime. Careers were generally closed to talent. These bourgeois, too, were nurtured in and conditioned by the critical, solvent, even subversive, ideas of the Enlightenment and of the *philosophes.* They were questioning the very foundations, arrangements and sanctions of society. Reform was in the air. Intelligent, educated, self-respecting, public-spirited and patriotic Frenchmen, particularly in the professions, were leading normal, useful, unexciting lives on the eve of the Revolution. Frustrated, too, they were ready for new institutions and for new values. The lawyers particularly were having experience with local, feudal and royal administration and being apprenticed for larger services during the Revolution.

In the town of Bernay in Normandy lived two brothers of a bourgeois family in easy circumstances who belonged to the group that steadily advocated reform. One was a doctor of theology of the Sorbonne and parish priest in his native town. The other was a lawyer. The priest was Robert-Thomas Lindet (1743–1823). The lawyer was Jean-Baptiste-Robert Lindet (1746–1825).[1] Constitutional monarchists at first, they were gradually won over by events to republicanism and remained staunch republicans to the end of their lives.

The brothers were devoted to each other and they enjoyed the intimacy of their closely-knit family. Robert Lindet was a bachelor

1. Sometimes confused, even by scholars, with his older brother because of the Robert common to their names. The older brother is usually known as Thomas and the younger always as Robert.

until he married in 1798 at fifty-three. The father was a respected wood and lumber merchant in Bernay, a town of 6,500. He and his wife, Marie-Anne Jouvin, "held an honorable place in the bourgeosie of the town."[2] The family was completed with a still younger brother, François, and a sister, Marie-Anne-Thereze. They lived in a house in the rue Saint-Vincent-de-Paul (now rue Thiers) facing the antiquated Maison de Charité.

Thomas Lindet was a delegate to the Estates-General in 1789 from the First Estate, a member of the National Constituent Assembly, constitutional bishop of the Department of the Eure, and a member of the Convention. Robert Lindet was *procureur du roi* in Bernay, revolutionary mayor of Bernay, member of the Legislative Assembly and of the Convention. His chief claim to fame in the Revolution was as a member of the Committee of Public Safety in the crisis years, 1793–94, responsible for provisioning and feeding the revolutionary armies and all of France. In this task he demonstrated zeal, devotion and extraordinary administrative talents.

These two brothers can be taken as representative of great numbers of other Frenchmen in the Revolution—sincere, honest, competent, incorruptible, moderate, staunch republicans. Thomas, the older, was a reforming priest, close to the members of his parish, and critical of the impiety and abuses of the higher clergy. As early as 1781, he advocated reforms in the Church, particularly for a more equitable distribution of ecclesiastical funds for the relief of the poor, for better remuneration of the priests, and for greater propriety in worship. In an address to the general assembly of his parish on November 4, 1781, he criticized the privileges of the higher clergy, the inequities suffered by the lower clergy, and the exorbitant funeral dues imposed on the poor. He spoke of the "excess of riches possessed by the honorary and supernumerary clergy." His own priestly income at the time was apparently 1,050 livres.[3] Thomas Lindet was indeed ready for thoroughgoing Church

---

2. Amand Montier (ed.), *Correspondance de Thomas Lindet, pendant la Constituante et la Législative (1789–1792)* (Paris: au siège de la Société de l'histoire de la Révolution Française, 1899), Introduction.

3. L. Boivin-Champeaux, *Notices Historiques sur la Révolution dans le Département de l'Eure* (Evreux: de l'imprimerie d'Auguste Herissey, 1868), pp. 68; 184–5.

reform in 1789. Amand Montier writes that the "political and social dream of Thomas Lindet was to reconcile the maxims of Christ with the principles of equality and of political liberty."[4] During the Revolution he was to display the courage of his convictions as well as considerable political sagacity.

Robert Lindet, the provincial lawyer, belonged, as Étienne Charavay puts it "to that able race of reforming jurists who demanded the convocation of the Estates-General and participated so actively in the hatching of the Revolution of 1789."[5] When he was named *procureur du roi* in Bernay in 1776 he became familiar with the complex fiscal and financial arrangements of the Old Regime, both feudal and royal. Montier writes that it "was in this harsh school that Robert Lindet acquired his solid understanding, his practical experience in administration that he used later so ably for the profit of his country." Many conditions, circumstances and first-hand experiences joined to groom this prudent, industrious, conscientious and firm Norman to be a consistent and moderate revolutionary in the stirring days ahead. Like his brother Thomas he had expressed his reforming ideas prior to the Revolution. In a speech on October 25, 1788, on the occasion of the restoration of the local *tribunal d'élection* he said: "We are in the expectation of an impending epoch which ought to be fertile in great events. All true citizens then should be eager to make all sacrifices that the sworn representatives of the nation believe to be necessary. We will be found, Messieurs, the most ardent to offer our positions, our abilities and our resources. May I be released soon from my responsibilities and see them better performed."[6]

Robert Lindet was a son of his times, a liberal bourgeois, enlightened by the *philosophes*, enamoured of the Roman Republic, and a sturdy provincial. As a lawyer, he was a member of the profession which was to provide the greatest number and the greatest leaders of the Revolution. Already middle-aged in 1789,

---

4. *Correspondance, op. cit.*, vii.
5. Amand Montier, *Robert Lindet, Député à L'Assemblée Législative et à la Convention, membre du Comité de Salut Public, Ministre des Finances, Notice Biographique* (Paris: Felix Alcan, Editeur, 1899), ii, Preface by Étienne Charavay.
6. *Ibid.*, pp. 2, 4.

he was maturing for the preferment that his fellow Normans were to give him in the years ahead. By 1789 both brothers, "equally devoted to the ideas of reform, enjoyed in the region a deserved popularity, due to the amenity of their relations and to the dignity of their private lives."[7]

The Lindets were not wealthy, although their circumstances were easy. Professor Palmer writes: "Lindet, Carnot and Prieur of the Côte-d'Or had fortunes approaching 50,000 livres before the Revolution."[8] Further evidence of the economic status of the Lindets was available early in the Revolution. By the decree of the National Assembly on October 6, 1789, all citizens were called upon for a *contribution patriotique* of one-fourth of their income. These contributions were to carry four percent interest, were payable in three installments, starting on April 1, 1790, and were to be redeemed. Robert Lindet in a declaration on March 7, 1790, stated that his loan of three hundred francs exceeded the percentage established by the decree. He also made a declaration for his father, fixing his contribution at five hundred francs.[9]

The ancient Duchy of Normandy nurtured the Lindet brothers. Bernay, their birthplace, was an old Celtic town. By the eve of the Revolution Normandy had a rich and diversified economy. The industrial revolution had been introduced from England and there were mills producing flannel and linen cloth and clothing. The land itself was, on the whole, fertile and productive. The substantial part of old Normandy that became the Department of the Eure in 1790 contained 603,700 hectares, divided into six great chalky plateaus, separated by pleasant valleys. The department got its name from the river Eure, which traversed it from south to north, flowing into the navigable Seine, which drained the Department. Smaller rivers were the Epte, Andelle, Risle, and the Charentonne, which flowed through Bernay. Evreux, the capital of the Department, was one hundred and eight kilometres west of Paris, or ten hours by post-stage. The region, because of its

7. Montier, *Correspondance, op. cit.*, iii.
8. R. R. Palmer, *Twelve Who Ruled: The Committee of Public Safety during the Terror* (Princeton: Princeton University Press, 1941), pp. 16–17. He explains that the purchasing power of the livre at the time resembled that of the dollar in 1940.
9. Montier, *Robert Lindet, op. cit.*, pp. 8–9.

nearness to the English Channel, had a moderate, temperate climate.

Arthur Young gives us a clear picture of the economy of Normandy in 1788. "They [the merchants of Rouen, in August, 1788] are right to have country villas, to get out of the great ugly, stinking, close, and ill-built town, which is full of nothing but dirt and industry . . . Rouen is dearer than Paris . . . The Parliament House here is shut up, and its members exiled a month past to their country seats, because they would not register the edict for a new land tax. I inquired much into the common sentiments of the people and found that the King personally, from having been here, is more popular than the parliament, to whom they attribute the dearness of everything." Later Young referred to Rouen as the Manchester of France. "All the way from Rouen . . . there is a scattering of country seats which I am glad to see; farmhouses and cottages everywhere, and the cotton manufacture in all."[10]

Normandy was indeed one of the great French industrial centers, particularly devoted to the production of cotton and woolen goods. Henri Sée speaks of industry in Normandy and its "farming out" by the town manufacturers. "In regions where agriculture was more prosperous, as in western Normandy, Picardy, and Flanders, the peasants engaged in rural industry were those with too little land to live from agriculture . . . There was no Norman village without its spinners and weavers. Some 180,000 persons were thus employed by the industry at Rouen." He later calls attention to the fact that the "industrial crisis wrought by the commercial treaty with England in 1786 caused extreme poverty among the workmen in the great industrial centers in eastern Normandy, Picardy, Flanders and Champagne."[11]

This treaty established a reciprocal low-tariff regime that favored the more industrially-advanced English manufacturers. Many in France attributed to it the great economic depression of 1787. The textile manufacturers of Rouen and Lyons felt particularly harmed.

10. Arthur Young, *Travels in France During the Years 1787, 1788, and 1789*, edited by Constantia Maxwell (Cambridge: Cambridge University Press, 1929), pp. 98–99.

11. Henri Sée, *Economic and Social Conditions in France During the Eighteenth Century*, translated by Edwin H. Zeydel (New York: Alfred A. Knopf, 1927), pp. 35, 213.

The Norman Chamber of Commerce protested the treaty and some in Normandy even urged war with England to rid themselves of it. It became patriotic to "buy French" and to dress in materials of French manufacture, known as *modes patriotiques*.[12]

Arthur Young calls attention to the abundant fruit trees in Normandy, to the well-stocked pastures, to the fine oxen being fattened for the Paris market, to the prevailing diet of buck-wheat, and to the fact that farms were as a rule larger than in much of France.[13] Sée points out that the holdings of the nobility in Normandy, Brittany and western France in general were larger than elsewhere but that the manorial system "seems to have been less onerous in Maine, Normandy and Champagne" than in other regions.[14]

Famines and food riots occurred in Normandy in the eighteenth century. One authority writes: "Even after 1750, when the value of property in France increased so greatly, there was no diminution in the number of bread riots. In Normandy alone the risings of 1752, 1764, 1766, 1767, and 1768 have become famous."[15] In the great grain famine of 1789, the Normans were driven to eat bread made of peas. A biographer of Thomas Lindet states that Bernay presented the "appearance of the blackest misery." He gives as one reason the frequent flooding of the Charentonne, which did much damage, made the town unhealthy, and destroyed its manufacturing.[16] Another writer, after mentioning the numerous and prosperous factories in Bernay, concludes: "Communications of the town with the outside being difficult one traveled little . . . Two days to go to Paris, and one needed to sleep at Evreux or at Mantes."[17] More attention will be given later to general

12. cf. Paul Mantoux, *The Industrial Revolution in the Eighteenth Century* (London: Jonathan Cape, 1961), new and revised edition, p. 257; Frances Acomb, *Anglophobia in France, 1763–1789: An Essay in the History of Constitutionalism and Nationalism* (Durham: Duke University Press, 1950), pp. 118–119; Georges Lefebvre, *La Grande Peur de 1789* (Paris: Société d'Edition d'Enseignement Supérieur, 1932), p. 14.

13. Young, *op. cit.*, pp. 108, 270, 283, 312.

14. Sée, *op cit.*, p. 23.

15. M. Roustan, *The Pioneers of the French Revolution* (London: Ernest Benn, Ltd., 1926), pp. 234–5.

16. Henry Turpin, *Thomas Lindet* (Bernay: Maison Duval, 1886), p. 5.

17. R. Meaulle, *Bernay Depuis Son Origine* (Bernay: Imprimerie Meaulle et Cie., n.d.), p. 23.

economic conditions in France in 1789 but it is not amiss to indicate here the disparity between the cost of living and wages. Jacques Bertrand points out that in France the "index of the cost of living increased by sixty-two percent from 1785 to 1789." Further, in the period from 1777 to 1793, the increase in wages was only sixteen percent, while from 1771 to 1789 the cost of living increased by forty-five percent, and the price of bread increased by fifty-eight to eighty-eight percent in various parts of France.[18]

With this historical heritage and in this physical setting the Lindet family found itself in the middle of the eighteenth century. Who were they, of what class, how did they educate their children, and what were their frustrations, their hopes, and their reasonable expectations? The brothers Lindet were not members of the upper bourgeoisie (*la haute bourgeoisie*) but of the middle bourgeoisie (*la bourgeosie moyenne*), an intelligent, well-read, highly-respected body of men, much less satisfied with the Old Regime than were the upper bourgeosie, and thus ready for leadership in the Revolution. Below this class were the *petite bourgeoisie*—tradespeople, craftsmen, clerks and lesser civil servants. Below them were *le peuple*, comprising probably ninety percent of the population—peasants of several grades, and the urban workers.

The role of the bourgeoisie in the eighteenth century and in the Revolution has become a favorite theme of students of the period. Georges Lefebvre writes that "it is no less true that the Revolution is but the crowning of a long economic and social revolution which has made the bourgeoisie the mistress of the world."[19] Jean Jaurès, in striking phrases, gives two great forces that made the Revolution possible: "From one side the French nation had arrived at intellectual maturity. From the other, the French bourgeoisie had arrived at social maturity." Relating this class to the germinal ideas of the Enlightenment, he continues: "All the vast informa-

---

18. Jacques Bertrand, *La Taxation des Prix sous la Révolution française* (Paris: Les Presses Continentales, 1949), p. 4, cf. John Lough, *An Introduction to Eighteenth Century France* (London: Longmans, Green & Co., Ltd., 1960), p. 43, for special reference to Normandy.

19. Georges Lefebvre, *Études sur la Révolution française* (Paris: Presses Universitaires de France, 1954), p. 246. First published in 1933 in *Cahiers de la Révolution française*.

tion and the generous philosophy of the eighteenth century would have been in vain had there not been a new social class interested in a profound change and capable of producing it. This social class is the bourgeoisie."[20]

Comprising the upper bourgeoisie were the financiers in the service of the king: bankers to the court, contractors and purveyers supplying the army and navy, and the great farmers-general. With them were the major crown officials—the civil service of the crown. Many of these had purchased their offices, some of which ennobled the bearer. Alongside these were the great bankers, merchants, rich industrialists, shipowners, as well as some distinguished artists and men of letters. Lefebvre says the "financiers were grand personages, allied by marriage with the aristocracy, cultivated men, sometimes learned, sometimes writers or patrons of the arts."[21] Members of this class often entered the ranks of the nobility by marriage or by the purchase of offices or by patents of nobility. The members of the Parlements, the *noblesse de robe*, were drawn from the bourgeoisie. The upper bourgeoisie "lived nobly." Professor Green writes that this rich and powerful group had become "virtually a governing class although it had no political power."[22] Elinor G. Barber attests to this in saying: "The power and influence of the financiers—farmers general and royal bankers —was indeed very great in this period when the French treasury relied on these private manipulators of wealth for its income. They had public functions without public responsibilities, and though the very great private profits they made as royal tax collectors were legitimate, their lack of responsibility nevertheless aroused much hostility as well as fear."[23]

Just below the upper level were the members of the liberal professions, among whom the lawyers of all kinds were the most numerous. Here one finds lesser government officials, judges of the lower courts, *procureurs, notaires, avocats*, the *receveurs des*

20. Jean Jaurès, *Les Causes économiques de la Révolution* (Paris: Bureau d'Editions Classiques Français de Socialisme, 1937), p. 27.
21. Georges Lefebvre, *The Coming of the French Revolution*, translated by R. R. Palmer (Princeton: Princeton University Press, 1947), p. 42.
22. F. C. Green, *The Ancien Regime: A Manual of French Institutions and Social Classes* (Edinburgh: Edinburgh University Press, 1958), p. 67.
23. Elinor G. Barber, *The Bourgeoisie in 18th Century France* (Princeton: Princeton University Press, 1955), pp. 29–30.

tailles and other ranking employees in internal revenue. The bourgeoisie, particularly those of the *bourgeoisie moyenne*, were men of the Enlightenment, educated by the *philosophes*, ready to abandon the historic, metaphysical and supernatural sanctions of the stagnant and anachronistic Old Regime.[24] Their intellectual and philosophical inclinations and their class interests combined to commit them to reform and change in the name of progress. Professor Lefebvre sums up this new outlook as follows: "The bourgeoisie put its emphasis on earthly happiness and on the dignity of man; it urged the necessity of increasing the former and elevating the latter, through the control of natural forces by science and the utilizing of them to augment the general wealth. The means, it was believed, consisted in granting entire freedom to investigation, invention and enterprise, for which the incentive was to be personal gain, or the charm of discovery, struggle and risk. The conception was dynamic, calling upon all men, without distinction of birth, to enter into a universal competition from which the progress of mankind was to follow without end."[25] Charles Morazé points out that the new notions, founded on reason, liberty and progress, challenged the hereditary permanence of the monarchial hierarchy at the very time that the traditional monarchy was approaching its apogee. "The triumph of reason," he writes,

24. For the influence of the *philosophes* and the Enlightenment in the conditioning of the Revolution and on the bourgeois revolutionaries see the following: Daniel Mornet, *La pensée française au XVIIIe siècle* (Paris: A. Colin, 1926); Henri Peyre, "The Influence of Eighteenth Century Ideas on the French Revolution," *Journal of the History of Ideas*, X (1949), pp. 63–87; Paul Hazard, *European Thought in the 18th Century: from Montesquieu to Lessing* (New Haven: Yale University Press, 1954); Charles Frankel, *The Faith of Reason: The Idea of Progress in the French Enlightenment* (New York: Columbia University Press, 1948); Alfred Cobban, *In Search of Humanity: The Role of the Enlightenment in Modern History* (New York: George Braziller, 1960), particularly pp. 161–179; 181–193; Gordon H. McNeil, "The Cult of Rousseau and the French Revolution," *Journal of the History of Ideas*, VI (1945), pp. 197–212; David T. Pottinger, *The French Book Trade in the Ancien Régime 1500–1791* (Cambridge: Harvard University Press, 1958), Ch. II, "The Author and His Public," for the increase in books in economics and political science published in the eighteenth century over the two preceding centuries; George R. Havens, *The Age of Ideas in 18th Century France* (New York: Henry Holt & Co., 1955).

25. *The Coming of the French Revolution, op. cit.,* pp. 48–49.

"was particularly welcomed by the bourgeoisie." Liberty for them meant freedom for economic progress, the suppression of restraints and of privileges, in the conviction that "if Privilege is usurpation, Property is an inviolable right." The twin supports of this thinking, stimulated by Voltaire, were "liberty, as a general concept inspired by economic liberty; property, the foundation of progress and of wealth."[26] Albert Soboul writes: "Those who work and produce are weighed down with burdens to preserve the privileged orders, those who possess the economic preponderance have no political rights. There lies the fundamental social contradiction of the *ancien* regime."[27] Certainly the bourgeosie wanted political power to protect and extend their economic interests, and power and prestige commensurate with their wealth and importance in the nation.

Professor Palmer in his *Twelve Who Ruled* describes the type represented by Robert Lindet, the principal subject of this present essay: "Lindet . . . was the oldest man of the twelve [members of the Committee of Public Safety, 1793–95]; C.-A. Prieur the youngest, except Saint-Just. All three in the 1780's were leading busy and undistinguished lives typical of the anonymous world that lies behind all revolutions." Palmer calls attention to the bourgeois character of the Great Committee and of the prosperity of several of its members, including Lindet. In addition to Lindet seven others were lawyers and "all twelve were intellectuals. They were steeped in the philosophy of the eighteenth century."[28]

While it is true that the middle bourgeoisie, including the *avocats*, were saturated with the ideas of the *philosophes*, Henri Peyre keeps the feet of the provincial *avocats* on the earthy ground of French common life. "The most thoroughgoing Revolutionaries had not, like Marx or Lenin, spent years in reading-rooms. They were petty lawyers in contact with the people, like Robespierre at Arras, veterinaries like Marat; in short, provincial men who knew the lives of the peasant, the artisan, and the humble country priest

26. Charles Morazé, *La France Bourgeoisie, XVIIIe–XXe Siècles* (Paris: Librairie Armand Colin, 1946), pp. 68–69, 71.
27. Albert Soboul, *La Révolution Française, 1789–1799* (Paris: Editions Sociales, 1948), pp. 19–20.
28. *Op cit.*, pp. 14, 18.

of France."[29] These sturdy roots are worth remembering. They are illustrated in the career and experiences of Robert Lindet. Montier attests to this when he writes: "provincial he was, provincial he remained . . . Norman, sagacious and prudent."[30]

The brothers Lindet received the kind of education common among the bourgeoisie of the period. Thomas was educated for the priesthood and earned the doctorate in theology at the Sorbonne. Robert was educated in the Faculty of Law in the University of Paris. Both had received their secondary schooling in the *collège* in Bernay. In their choices of profession they illustrate what their contemporary A. C. Thibaudeau wrote in his *Mémoires*: "Two major careers were open to the bourgeoisie: the Church and the law courts. It regarded commerce and industry as a derogation."[31]

Education in eighteenth-century France was virtually a monopoly of the Church, from the primary schools through the universities.[32] Approximately one-hundred of the 562 secondary schools (*collèges*) were in the hands of the Jesuits until they were expelled from the schools in 1762 and banished from France in 1764. The rest were administered and taught by other teaching Orders of the Church, and of these the Oratoriens were the most important and progressive. Excepting for their schools, secondary education was almost completely classical and quite inadequate for life in

29. Henri Peyre, "The Influence of Eighteenth Century Ideas on the French Revolution," *Journal of the History of Ideas*, X (1949), pp. 67–68.

30. *Robert Lindet, op. cit.*, p. 16.

31. A. C. Thibaudeau, *Biographie. Mémoires, 1765–1792* (Paris: H. Champion, 1875), p. 53.

32. For education in the eighteenth century see Albert Drury, *L'Instruction Publique et la Révolution* (Paris: Librairie Hachette et Cie., 1882); H. C. Barnard, *The French Tradition in Education* (Cambridge: Cambridge University Press, 1922); Paul Lacroix, *Le XVIIIe Siècle—Institutions, Usages et Coutumes* (Paris: Librairie de Firmin-Didot Frères, Fils et Cie., 1875); Harold T. Parker, *The Cult of Antiquity and the French Revolutionaries. A Study in the Development of the Revolutionary Spirit* (Chicago: University of Chicago Press, 1937); Alphonse Aulard, *Études et Leçons sur La Révolution Française* (Quatrième série, 2me éd; Paris: Felix Alcan, Editeur 1908), I, "L'Education scolaire des hommes de la Révolution;" L'Abbé Augustin Sicard, *L'Education Morale et Civique Avant et Pendant La Révolution* (Paris: Librairie Poussielgue, 1884); Francis Delbeke, *L'Action Politique et Sociale des Avocates aux XVIIIe Siècle* (Louvain: Librairie Universitaire, 1927); Frederick E. Farrington, *French Secondary Schools* (London: Longmans, Green & Co., 1910).

the eighteenth century. Little attention was given to French history and literature, and little, if any, to mathematics and the sciences.

The bourgeois leaders of the Revolution were naturally conditioned by this standard education. Their speeches on the floor of the revolutionary assemblies are full of classical allusions, particularly to the Roman Republic, which they glorified. They regarded "Republican Rome as a liberal's dream," writes Harold T. Parker, and Henri Peyre goes so far as to write of their "myth of the ancients and their passion for liberty and virtue."[33]

At the apex of the educational system were the twenty-one universities. The greatest and most ancient was the University of Paris, with its four Faculties of Arts, Law, Medicine and Theology, and its virtual control over the *collèges* in Paris. The University, however, was in a state of decline and had ceased to be important in the intellectual and cultural life of the nation. The universities had indeed become citadels of privilege, tradition and authority, if not of reaction.

Robert Lindet's preparation for a career in law was about as classical and as outmoded as had been his secondary education. Subjects were taught in Latin excepting for French law, and were taught quite mechanically. The three branches of law studied were Roman, Canon, and French. Little attention was paid to the history and principles of the law. In fact, the law faculty had almost become a trade school to prepare practitioners of the law. Canon law was important for all lawyers because of the confusion and overlapping of civil and ecclesiastical jurisdictions.[34]

The title of *Licencié ès Lois* was granted at the end of the three-year course and the successful defense of a thesis. After receiving the degree and taking the oath the new *avocat* needed two or three years of practice before he could be registered on the roll (*inscrit au tableau*). Persons so inscribed gained a precedence among the liberal professions, although, of course, inferior to the magistracy (*noblesse de robe*). There was a great variety

33. Parker, *The Cult of Antiquity, op. cit.*, pp. 26–27; Peyre, "The Influence of Eighteenth Century Ideas on the French Revolution," *op. cit.*, p. 82.

34. See Francis Delbeke, *L'Action Politique et Sociale des Avocats*, etc., *op. cit.*, for an illuminating description of legal education in the eighteenth century.

of meanings attached to the title "avocat" as well as in the regulations of the bar. Voltaire defined the word avocat ironically in the *Dictionnaire philosophique*: "An avocat is a person who, not having enough fortune to buy one of the brilliant offices [magistracies] so prominent in the public eye, studied the laws of Theodosius and Justinian for three years in order to understand the custom [*coutume*] of Paris, and who, finally, being registered, had the right to plead for fees, if he had a strong voice."[35]

In the administration of justice in the eighteenth century, customary law generally prevailed in northern France and Roman law in the south. Ordinary justice of the king was administered in three types of courts. First, the Parlements or High Courts of Appeal of which there were thirteen, and four royal Councils with similar judicial functions. These courts were manned by the nobility of the robe. The Parlement of Paris dated from 1302 and that of Rouen from 1499. Secondly, the *présideaux*, of which there were about one hundred, which judged all criminal cases too unimportant for the Parlements, and civil actions involving less than 2,000 francs. Finally, there were bailiwick courts, seneshal courts, and provotships, the last (*prévôtés*) in Normandy were called viscounty (*vicomtés*). In addition there were the seigneurial, or feudal, courts, each with a judge, lord's attorney, clerk, and jailer.

The Bar of Rouen had an old and honorable history and was well-organized. It operated under strict and severe professional regulations dating from the fifteenth century. In 1692 these were summarized in twenty-three articles by the General Assembly of the Order for the "maintenance of good discipline in the Bar and in the profession." These regulations were renewed in 1768 and in 1782 and in 1785 they were revised. Although the Bar of Rouen was proud and jealous of its prerogatives and often had to struggle for its rights against the Parlement of Normandy, it strongly supported the Parlement against royal power. When Louis XV suppressed the Parlement in 1772 the Bar overwhelmingly refused to plead before the *Conseil Supérieure* and a few of the most outspoken *avocats* were arrested and exiled. The Parlement was re-

---

35. Quoted in Louis Ducros, *La Société française au dix-huitième* (2me. éd., Paris: Librairie A. Hatier, 1933), p. 144.

The *avocats* again boycotted the new jurisdiction during the exile of the Parlement. Those who demanded the restoration of the Parlement also demanded the restoration of the provincial estates of Normandy, which had been abolished in 1655.[36]

Many *avocats* in Normandy, however, deplored the unwillingness of the Parlement and the other courts to assume leadership in the reorganization of the judiciary and in the reform of ancient abuses in the laws, their administration, and the antiquated and cruel penalties and punishments imposed. Jacques-Guillaume Thouret, a leading *avocat* of Rouen and a future president of the National Constituent Assembly, was one of the ablest advocates of these reforms. It is a fact that the Parlements were essentially interested only in the defense of their own prerogatives and vested interests *vis à vis* the king, and not in the reform of the laws or of the Old Regime.

"Judges and *procureurs* were, in general," writes Jacques Godechot, "little loved, they were the implacable defenders of a state of affairs favorable to their interests, but which the majority of the French believed to be outmoded. Only the *avocats*, recruited from the *moyenne*, even the *petite bourgeoisie*, approved judicial reform and often even were its advocates. A violent campaign disturbed the land from 1760 in favor of the reorganization of justice, in which the influence of Voltaire, Montesquieu and Beccaria was marked." Albert Guerard and Francis Delbeke write to the same effect and Franklin L. Ford remarks that the "attitude of sovereign court judges toward the *avocats* seems generally to have been at best one of condescension and at worst one of contempt."[37]

Henri Sée links the bourgeoisie as a group with the *avocats*: "It is the bourgeoisie which instigated the revolutionary move-

36. For the law and the courts in Normandy, see: M. Houard, *Dictionnaire analytique, historique, Etymologique, critique et interprétatif De la Coutume de Normandie* (4. vols., Rouen: Chez le Boucher, 1780); Adolphe Joanne, *Géographie du Département de l'Eure*, (Paris: Librairie Hachette et Cie., 1896); Albert Sarrazin, *Le Barreau de Rouen, hier et aujourd'hui* (Rouen: Imprimerie de Léon Brière, 1899).

37. Jacques Godechot, *Les Institutions de la France sous la Révolution et l'Empire* (Paris: Presses Universitaires de France, 1951, p. 110; Albert Guerard, *The Life and Death of an Ideal—France in the Classical Age* (London: W. H. Allen, 1957, Ch. 5; Delbeke, *op. cit.*, pp. 118, 283, 301; Franklin L. Ford, *Robe and Sword: The Regrouping of the French Aristocracy after Louis XIV* (Cambridge: Harvard University Press, 1953), p. 37.

ment, that was its initiator. Profound causes explain this. This class had an interest in a new order of things; in a more regular organization, in the destruction of the privileges of the first two orders, and in the recognition of civil equality. It felt itself qualified by its education and abilities to take the government in hand. The *avocats*, these men of the law, knew admirably and in detail the abuses of the administration, and of the social organization; they could propose a precise program of reform. They would be content, no doubt, with a transformation which would give satisfaction to their class, without touching too directly the regime of property." Sée concludes by returning to the whole class: "For the bourgeoisie the interests of their class was blended with those of humanity, and it was indeed the progress of humanity of which the revolutionaries thought . . . But their idealism, no more than was the philosophy of the eighteenth century, was not an abstract conception, a mystical sentiment [but] it corresponded to the specific reform of particular abuses, of which one had experience and from which one suffered daily."[38]

Robert Lindet was a member of this important and enlightened order of *avocats*, practicing in his native town. On September 11, 1776, he was named *procureur du roi près le tribunal de l'élection de Bernay.* In this office he became familiar with fiscal and financial matters, the assessment of the *taille, aides* and other taxes of the royal treasury. Thus for thirteen years before the Revolution he was working with administration in the Old Regime and aware of its limitations and obsolescence. By 1789 he had more than served his apprenticeship as an administrator on a small scale in a limited sphere.

Turning from Robert the lawyer to Thomas the priest one asks what caused the latter to become a reforming priest within the Church and, finally, an active revolutionary. The question suggests a brief survey of the Church in the eighteenth century. It was divided into 135 dioceses. There were about 130,000 members of the clergy, or the First Estate, on the eve of the Revolution. Ten to eleven thousand of these were the upper clergy, which included the archbishops, bishops, vicar-generals, cathedral and collegiate stored by Louis XVI in 1774 but was suppressed again in 1788.

38. Henri Sée, *La Vie Economique et les Classes Sociales en France au XVIIIe Siècle* (Paris: Librairie Felix Alcan, 1924), pp. 173–4.

canons, priors and abbots. In 1789 all the archbishops and bishops were of the nobility, and many other members of the upper clergy were of noble families, often younger sons. The wealthier archbishops and bishops were usually absent from their dioceses, residing in Paris or Versailles. There were roughly 60,000 members of the lower secular clergy, and about the same number of monks and nuns comprising the regular clergy. It is estimated that there were at least 3,000 religious houses of the various orders in France in 1789.[39]

The Church was wealthy. It imposed tithes on all parishes and on all classes. It enjoyed great revenues from its vast properties. Some of its "princes" received high incomes. The Bishop of Strasbourg had an annual income of 400,000 livres from his diocese and 130,000 livres from abbeys which he held in commendation. Other bishops had incomes of 100,000 to 200,000 livres, though the average episcopal income did not exceed thirty to forty thousand livres. Some of the bishops were quite poor. Professor Palmer speaks of the Church as a "rich, powerful, and closely organized corporation . . . It was backed by the leading families of France, and was entrenched in the whole family system . . . It disturbed the country by the intrigue, rivalry, and theological rancor of its clergy. A public power in its own right, it entered into secular politics, swaying the minds or demanding the aid of servants of the crown. Through its parish organization, its schools, almshouses, and literary publications, it exercised over everyone in France an influence independent both of public opinion and of civil authority."[40]

The clergy were exempt from state taxation but the Assembly of the Clergy periodically, usually every five years, voted the *décimes*, from a part of which they gave a *don gratuit* or voluntary gift to the Crown. This was very substantially less than taxes on its properties would have been. The clergy were charged with the

---

39. For religion and the Church see: Abbé Joseph Lacoutre, *La Politique Religieuse De La Révolution* (Paris: Editions Auguste Picard, 1940); R. R. Palmer, *Catholics and Unbelievers in 18th Century France* (Princeton: Princeton University Press, 1939); André Latraille, *L'Eglise Catholique et la Révolution Française. Le Pontificat de Pie VI et la crise française, 1775–1799* (Paris: Librairie Hachette, 1946).

40. *Catholics and Unbelievers*, etc., *op. cit.*, p. 5.

responsibility for registering births, baptisms, marriages and deaths, for public assistance and charity, and had a virtual monopoly over education. The monastic orders were generally in a degenerate state in the middle of the century. A Commission for the Regular Clergy was appointed by the Assembly of the Clergy in 1765 and this Commission vigorously reformed the orders in the years prior to the Revolution.

The *curés*, or parish priests, such as Thomas Lindet, were the ones who really served the religious needs of the great majority of the French people, as they went about on their "errands of faith and mercy." Excepting in the few great cities they lived close to their parishioners and shared the meagerness of their lives. Many of these priests were not well-educated, particularly in the rural areas. Most were simple, sincere and devout persons, respected and trusted by the peasants and workers. They were very poor. In 1768 their annual stipend was raised from three hundred to five hundred francs, and in 1786 to seven hundred and fifty francs. The *curés* were appointed to their parishes either by the bishop, by the superior of an abbey, or by lay patrons of livings. A social gulf separated them from the highly privileged upper clergy. Professor Gershoy writes that the relations between these two levels were "an exchange of arrogance on the one part and open or suppressed hostility on the other."[41]

The Marquis de Ferrières describes in his *Mémoires* the members of the clergy in the Estates-General, composed overwhelmingly of *curés*, who "detested equally the bishops and the nobles, and secretly desired to unite with the Third Estate." André Latraille says that by 1789 the clergy were "too divided, too uncertain, too *gangrené* . . . to hold the country, in case of grave crisis, to fidelity to the traditional religion." Of the 300 representatives of the First Estate in the States-General, 208 were *curés*, mostly from rural parishes, forty-seven bishops, and thirty-five abbés. The *curés* "arrived, their feelings still vibrant from the animation of the electoral debates."[42]

41. *The French Revolution, op. cit.,* p. 33.
42. Marquis de Ferrières, Charles-Elie, *Mémoires pour Servir à l'histoire de l'Assemblée Constituante de la Révolution de 1789* (22 vols., Paris: Les Marchands de Nouveautés, An VII), I, p. 40; André Latraille, *L'Eglise Catholique*, etc., *op. cit.*, I, p. 26.

Thomas Lindet was one of these parish priests chosen to represent his Order in the Estates-General. He had steadily advocated reform in the Church. He was *curé* of the parish of Sainte-Croix in Bernay, then in the diocese of Lisieux. His church dated from 1374 and during his incumbency had 4,000 communicants. The diocese of Evreux at this time had 550 parishes and contained sixteen abbeys, eleven of men and five of women.

Thomas Lindet, the reforming priest, and Robert Lindet, the practical *avocat* and administrator with a civic sense, were ready for the calling of the Estates-General and the advent of the Revolution. In 1789 Thomas was forty-six and Robert was two years younger. Their age helps to account for the balance and moderateness of their behavior in the Revolution but it also perhaps increased the depth and sincerity of their convictions.

CHAPTER TWO

Thomas Lindet in the National Constituent Assembly

THE TEN MONTHS prior to the convening of the Estates-General on May 5, 1789, were alive with political thought, criticism and activity. The Order in Council of July 5, 1788, requesting information and suggestions concerning the historic Estates-General—which had not met since 1614—set off an explosion of pamphlets and sparked vigorous discussions throughout France. The local and bailiwick assemblies meeting to elect deputies to the Estates-General focussed attention on the choosing of men to represent the Orders and the nation in the governmental emergency. The needs, demands and hopes of the people were forcefully expressed in the *cahiers* drafted by these assemblies, to be carried by the deputies to the Estates-General.

Louis XVI, driven by the impending bankruptcy of the Government, by the unwillingness of the Assembly of the Notables to suggest any remedies, and by the failure of his ministers to propose any other expedients or possibilities, issued his Royal Letter of Convocation on January 24, 1789, calling for the meeting of the Estates-General on April 27 (later changed to the first week in May) in Versailles.

"Our beloved and faithful, we need the cooperation of our loyal subjects in surmounting all our financial difficulties and in establishing, according to our wishes, a constant and invariable order in all branches of the government which affect the welfare of our subjects and the prosperity of our Kingdom. Such worthy motives have induced us to convene the assembly of the estates of all the provinces of our dominion to advise us and assist us in whatever is presented to them and to inform us of the wishes and grievances of our people, so that . . . an efficacious remedy for the ills of the State may be obtained as promptly as possible, and abuses of every sort reformed and prevented by safe and sound methods which will assure public felicity and will restore to us in particular the peace and tranquillity whereof we have been deprived for so long."[1]

This amiable letter was followed by regulations of the same date, outlining in detail the procedures for the elections. They were to take place in from two to four steps, according to region and district, each in an assembly of qualified voters and electors. For the Third Estate payment of some tax, direct or indirect, was pre-requisite to voting. The rural suffrage was nearly universal. It had been decided on December 27, 1788, that the Third Estate would have as many representatives as the other two Orders com-bined. No decision was reached on the question of meeting and voting, whether by Orders, or together.

More than a thousand pamphlets were published between Jan-uary 1788 and June 1789. The liberal "Patriots" and their steer-ing "Committee of Thirty" took the lead in the educational and propaganda campaign throughout the country, both in pamphlets and petitions, and vocally in the academies, Masonic societies, clubs, reading circles, cafes, and salons. All these activities con-tributed greatly to the intensive education of the French in the issues at stake, in the prevailing philosophic ideas, and suggested ideological and practical means whereby the interests of the nation might be served. The pamphlets had great influence on the *cahiers* that were prepared in the various electoral assemblies during the early spring of 1789.[2] Professor Shafer, calling attention to the bourgeois nationalism in these pamphlets, characterizes them succinctly as follows: "Reflective of the dominant bourgeois ideals of the time, they advocate a society based on liberty and prosper-

1. John Hall Stewart, *A Documentary Survey of the French Revolution* (New York: The Macmillan Co., 1951), pp. 29–30.
2. See Beatrice Hyslop, *A Guide to the General Cahiers of 1789, with the Texts of Unedited Cahiers* (New York: Columbia University Press, 1936), pp. 62ff.

ity, to be achieved through patriotism and realized in a national
state."[3]

Leading Normans, particularly the *avocats*, participated in this
spontaneous campaign of pamphleteering. Jacques-Guillaume
Thouret, the distinguished *avocat* of Rouen and later president of
the National Constituent Assembly,[4] composed a pamphlet, *Avis
des bons Normands à leurs frères tous les bons français de toutes
les provinces et de tous les ordres* (1789). "Respectable citizens,
do not refuse us your attention. We speak to you in the name of
the nation. It is the question of your happiness, of your prosperity,
of the honor and the security of France." He named the two great
enemies of all Frenchmen as the "hydra of abuses originating in
the financial disorder and the disastrous mistakes of the government when it is too perplexed in its policies."[5]

The *avocats* of Normandy boldly addressed the king in 1788
in a *Mémoire présenté au roi par les avocats au parlement de
Normandie* in which they said: "We have the honor to point out
to your Majesty that no order of citizens is able to exist outside
the nation or, existing in the nation, is able to upset the balance
or destroy the unity of the social entity."[6] The *avocats* of the
Bailiwick of Orbec-Bernay sent a petition to the Director-General
of Finances on November 3, 1788, presenting their views "concerning the composition of the Estates-General." They pled for
the representation of the Third Estate equal to that of the other
two Orders combined, but made no recommendation concerning
the method of meeting or voting. Robert Lindet was one of the
eleven signers, another being Jean-Michel DuRoy—later a member
of the Convention and executed as a regicide in 1795 in the
Thermidorian Reaction.[7]

The *Généralité* of Rouen was composed of four major baili-

3. Boyd C. Shafer, "Bourgeois Nationalism in the Pamphlets on the Eve
of the French Revolution," *The Journal of Modern History*, Vol. X, No. 1,
March 1938, p. 31.
4. Jacques-Guillaume Thouret (1746–1794) was executed in the Terror
on the accusation of Couthon that he was an accomplice of Danton.
5. Quoted in Shafer, *op. cit.*, pp. 32, 34.
6. *Ibid.*, p. 38.
7. Archives Nationales, Biii 65, Collection Générale des Procès-Verbaux,
Mémoires, Lettres et autres pièces concernant les Députations à L'Assemblée
Nationale en 1789, Tome LXV, Bailly d'Evreux, Seconde Partie., 445.

wicks: Rouen, Evreux, Caux à Cadabec, and Chaumont-en-Vexin. The first of these was to elect sixteen deputies to the Estates-General, the second eight, the third twelve, and the last four. Orbec-Bernay was a secondary bailiwick to Evreux, electing its representatives to the General Assembly at Evreux.[8] On the authority of M. Le Danois de la Loisière, Lieutenant-General of the Bailiwick of Bernay and mayor of the town, and of Robert Lindet, *Procureur* of the King in the Bailiwick, the call was issued on February 27, 1789, for the meeting of the General Assembly of the Third Estate of the Bailiwick on March 9 at eight o'clock in the morning in one of the halls of the Abbey of Bernay.[9] According to the *procès-verbal* of the Assembly the deputies met on March 9 at the appointed hour in the Great Hall of the Royal Abbey of the town. Robert Lindet's was the first signature on the minutes of the meeting. The deputies met through March 11. It is apparent from the records that Robert Lindet was active in the deliberations of the Assembly, as his brother Thomas seems to have been in the Assembly of the First Estate. Both became delegates to the General Assembly in Evreux.

When the representatives assembled in Bernay on March 9 they brought with them the *cahiers* from the villages and parishes. These were organized and edited into one *cahier* by a committee of sixteen of which Robert Lindet was a member. This *cahier* was adopted unanimously on March 11 by the Assembly, which gave its four elected delegates to the General Assembly the power to represent the *cahier* fully at Evreux in all that "concerned the needs of the state, the reform of abuses, the establishment of a fixed and durable order in all parts of the administration, the prosperity of the Kingdom and the welfare of all and of each of the subjects of His Majesty."[10]

The *Cahier* of this secondary Bailiwick of Orbec-Bernay, like the others from the various levels of assemblies in France, is very illuminating in its revelation of the conditions and state of mind

---

8. Armand Brette, *Les Constituents* (Paris: Société de l'Histoire de la Révolution Française, 1897), pp. 93–97.

9. Archives Départmentales de l'Eure.

10. Archives Départmentales de l'Eure. (Evreux), Procès verbal d'assemblée de M.M. les Députés de l'Ordre du Tiers-État du Bailliage d'Orbec-Bernay. 9–11 Mars, 1789.

of the times. In introducing the eight main headings of the *Cahier*
the Assembly expressed itself as "eager to consecrate its earliest
enthusiasm, hope and enlightened reason to its sovereign, the
sacrifice of all its powers and all its faculties in order to uphold
the authority of the monarch, and contribute to the increase of
his powers."[11] The Assembly then proceeded to plunge into the
concrete grievances and proposals of the *Cahier*. It criticized the
exemptions and privileges of the nobles, rooted in feudalism, and
called for the proportional contribution of the nobility and the
clergy to the support of the state.

It proclaimed that the convocation of the Estates-General was
not to be considered as an accidental event, but was to be bound
inseparably with the administration as a fundamental principle of
government; that the Estates-General should vote appropriations
only for the period of one Assembly and that the collections would
cease at the time determined by the next Assembly, if the Estates
did not approve new revenues; that the law should guarantee the
periodic meetings of the Estates; that the provincial estates should
be re-activated after their suspension of 150 years; that the King
be supplicated to regulate the expenses of his household in conformity with the *éclat* and the grandeur due to the most powerful
monarch in Europe, while at the same time establishing plans of
reform and of economy in all departments; the King should
abolish the militia and all forms of forced service, for the people
looked upon service in the militia as oppression excepting in the
case of threatened invasion when "every citizen becomes a soldier."

The *Cahier* urged one tax only upon property, to apply to all
in the same proportion without distinction; that the Estates maintain the individual liberty of citizens, the freedom of commerce,
of the arts, of agriculture, and of the numerous class of citizens
who were employed; and that the Third Estate remain inviolably
united to the Papacy in the profession of the same faith and in the
practice of the same morality. There were many detailed articles
on the Church and its hierarchy and on justice and the courts. The
Church's maladministration of charity was criticised and the

11. Archives Nationales, Biii 65, *op. cit.*, Cahier des Doléances, Instructions et Pouvoir des Habitans composant le Tiers-État du Bailliag ed'Orbec-
Bernay—11 Mars 1789, pp. 531–597.

troubles and miseries of the *curés* emphasized. In the administration of justice attention was called to the overlapping and confusion of jurisdictions between the town, feudal and ecclesiastical courts in Bernay. The revocation of all *lettres de cachet* was called for. No one should be detained excepting by virtue of a legal judgment and all prisoners should be restored to the processes of ordinary justice. Liberty of the press should be established and maintained as a constitutional right. Laws should be promulgated with the greatest amount of publicity. The *Cahier* declared that these fundamental principles should be agreed upon by the Estates-General before it concerned itself with the public debt.

This brief résumé barely does justice to the well-informed, comprehensive and vigorous presentation of grievances and proposals for reform. The provincials responsible for the *Cahier* were self-respecting, enlightened, aroused and hopeful citizens.

The Lieutenant-General of the Bailiwick of Bernay reported the sessions of this Assembly of the Third Estate to the Keeper of the Seals on March 12, 1789, saying that it had deliberated with great "wisdom and zeal" and that the wishes of the members steadily "breathed love and gratitude to the King, and the most respectful confidence in the paternal intentions of His Majesty, and in the virtuous, frank and patriotic plans of his ministers," and expressed an "unlimited devotion to the public welfare."[12] The Lieutenant-General enclosed a copy of the *Procès-Verbal* of the Assembly, and a copy of its *Cahier*. He himself was elected to the General Assembly at Evreux. Fifteen others were elected, including Robert Lindet and M. Solin, dean of the *avocats* of Bernay. The Assembly of Clergy of the same Bailiwick elected, among others, Thomas Lindet, *curé* of Sainte-Croix, and LeBertre, *curé* of Notre Dame de la Couture in Bernay, to the Assembly of the Three Orders in Evreux. It is surely apparent by these elections that the two brothers, both of them liberals, were respected and trusted leaders in their own community.

The Assembly of the Third Estate met in Evreux between March 17 and 24, 1789. François de Girardin, Lieutenant-General of the major Bailiwick of Evreux, presided. Robert Lindet was named one of the five commissioners from the Bailiwick of Bernay

12. *Ibid.*, pp. 528–9.

to edit the *cahiers* brought to the Assembly from the secondary bailiwicks. There were thirty-six on the Commission, including De Girardin, Le Danois de la Loisière, Buzot (elected a deputy to the Estates-General and, later, to the Convention where he was a leading Girondin, a victim of the purge of the Girondins in the spring of 1793).

The municipal officers of Evreux memorialized the King on the occasion of the General Assembly of the Three Orders meeting in their city. They acknowledged with "tender emotion and respectful gratitude" the call of the King for the Estates-General, saying that its restoration "will be one of the most glorious epochs of the reign of Your Majesty, a truly happy event since it is born in the midst of our misfortunes." The memorial went on to summarize the financial crisis of the state and the burdens imposed upon the people. It spoke of the Third Estate and its rights. Reflecting the ideas of the *philosophes* it called these "inviolable rights because they are founded on nature conforming to reason and to good order . . . The Third Estate owes to Your Majesty the fulfilment of these rights, unknown for centuries . . . Sire, the Third Estate is not at all as it has been represented to Your Majesty, as ambitious, turbulent, inconsiderate, and an insatiable disturber, in its pretensions. Your Majesty has a more just and true opinion than that. It asks only to be reintegrated in that portion of liberty natural to man and of which no power has the right to despoil him; it only reclaims the rights that flow from this original and constitutional nature of his being; it believes that in the enlightened century in which we live, kings recognize the limits of their authority, choosing by preference the power that brings justice and reason, preferring to govern free subjects rather than to lead an enslaved people."[13]

The memorial continued in very humane terms to beg the King to alleviate the miseries of great numbers of indigent artisans and workers so that their misfortunes would no longer consume them. "Your Majesty, take under your protection this unfortunate class

13. Arch. Nat'l. Biii, 64. Table Chronologique des actes relatifs à la Convocation et à la Députation du Bailliage d'Evreux et autres Secondaires aux États-Généraux de 1789, Addresse de remerciement presentée au Roi, par les officiers municipaux de la ville d'Evreux, en Assemblée générale. The address is signed but is without date.

and put an end to its suffering. It is from them that you will receive, Sire, the most moving benedictions for your tender heart and its accomplishment will reap for you forever the sweet name of father of the people . . ."

The Three Orders met both separately and together at Evreux. When they sat together it was in the ancient Cathedral, consecrated first in 1072 by Lanfranc. The *procès-verbal* of the General Assembly lists the names of the members, by Orders, the deputies elected by each of the Orders to the Estates-General, and the *cahiers* of each Order. There is also the report of deputations of each Order to the others, their messages and addresses to each other, and the courtesy and attention with which these were received.

Within the First Estate matters were not so harmonious. The Bishop of Evreux, who presided over the Assembly of the Clergy, assisted by the Bishop of Lisieux, sent a letter to the Keeper of the Seals on March 20, 1789, in which the cleavage within the Order is explicit. "The great number of *curés,* who came in a spirit of cabal, brought trouble and division." He went on to detail their activities, their clandestine meetings and their grievances against the bishops. "I proposed the name of a secretary, but my proposal was rejected with the greatest indecency. We want such a *curé,* they said . . . They manage always to achieve the most injurious influence over the rights of the rest of the Clergy . . . Everything that the Bishop of Lisieux and I proposed was immediately rejected with the most marked misunderstanding." The two bishops wanted to restrict the grievances (*doléances*) to matters concerning religion and the state, but the *curés* insisted on including the administrative and financial problems of the Church and of all the clergy.[14]

The *Cahier* of the Third Estate was adopted on March 23.[15] There were ninety-three articles in all. The final article is a summary of principles. The *Cahier* requested double the number of representatives for the Third Estate; that the Orders reserve the freedom to assemble and to deliberate separately or in common;

14. Arch. Nat'l. Biii, 65, pp. 32–36.
15. Arch. Nat'l., Biii, 64. Des Déliberations de l'Ordre du Tiers-État arrêtées à l'Assemblée Générale du Bailliage d'Evreux, le 23 Mars, 1789, pp. 398–420.

that before any deliberation, it be agreed that a fundamental charter assure to France a good and solid constitution under which it would be recognized by law that the legislative powers would reside essentially in the concurrence of the people in assembly and the authority of the king; that the Estates-General meet at fixed and regular times; that provincial Estates be re-esablished in all the kingdom; that no restraint under any pretext be put upon the individual liberty of the citizen; that religious liberty be guaranteed; that non-Catholics enjoy all the rights of citizens and their civil status be guaranteed by the Estates-General.

The *Cahier* continued its marshalling of demands: all unequally assessed taxes were to be suppressed as well as all pecuniary privileges, and only those taxes adopted by the three Orders and borne equally would be legal; no taxes were to be imposed except by the free and unanimous consent of the three Orders; the wisest precautions were to be taken to prevent excessive prices for grain; the question of the uniformity of weights and measures throughout the kingdom was to be examined; the Estates-General should find a rule to harmonize the unlimited freedom and the regulation of the arts, commerce and industry. The *Cahier* was explicit in Article XXXIX: "That the Estates-General concern itself with efficacious means of remedying the disadvantages which have resulted in the Province of Normandy from the Treaty of Commerce made with England; also, that the Estates-General study whether the machines for combing cotton are injurious or advantageous to the nation, that internal tariffs be abolished and that the freedom of circulation and transportation be assured in the entire kingdom; that seignorial feudal rights and monopolies be abolished; that the King be supplicated to stop the abuse of the plurality of benefices; that the lot of the *curés* and vicars be ameliorated; that as soon as possible schools of all kinds be established in the cities and free primary schools in the towns and in the country; that the militia and forced labor be abolished; that the Third Estate be not excluded from any military rank and that commerce is to be open to the nobility without derogation." There was also much on the reform of laws and the courts.

This *Cahier*, like the one from the Third Estate of the secondary Bailiwick of Orbec-Bernay, gives a good picture of conditions in

Normandy and the readiness of the representatives of the people for basic reforms and changes in the constitutional, economic, ecclesiastic and social structure of the nation.

The General Assembly was to send eight deputies to the Estates-General, four from the Third Estate and two from each of the other two Estates. The two from the Clergy were Jean-Jacques de la Lande, *curé* of d'Illiers-l'Evêque,[16] and Thomas Lindet. Both were thus from the lower clergy. The two representing the nobility were Nicholas, comte de Bonneville, a retired lieutenant-colonel, and Louis-François, Marquis de Chambray, *maréchal de camp*, chevalier de Saint-Louis, and honorable Knight of Malta.[17] The four from the Third Estate were Pierre-Joseph-Antoine Beauperry, horse dealer, Adrien-George Buschey des Noës, *conseiller du roi et de Monsieur* in the Bailiwick of Bernay,[18] François-Nicholas Buzot, and Denis Lemaréchal, merchant.[19]

The Third Estate elected 577 deputies to the Estates-General, of whom more than half were lawyers. The deputies of the First Estate included ninety-four great prelates and nearly two hundred parish priests. Outstanding among the lawyers were Target, Tronchet, Camus, Le Chapelier, Mounier, Merlin de Douai, Barnave, Barère, Robespierre, Lanjuinais, and the two Normans, Buzot and Thouret. Abbé Siéyès, elected by the Third Estate, was influential in the early stages of the Assembly, and Mirabeau, of the nobility but also elected by the Third Estate, was a dominating figure. There were a few liberal higher clergy such as Abbé Grégoire and Talleyrand, Bishop of Autun. There were also some liberal nobles such as Adrien Duport, Charles de Lameth, the Duc de La Rochefoucault-Liancourt, and Lafayette, who had a large and hopeful following.

The opening days of the Estates-General were inauspicious because of the ineptitude of the King and Necker, and their failure to present a positive program to give direction and leader-

16. A monarchist, he was imprisoned in Paris and massacred September 3, 1792.

17. He emigrated to Vienna during his term and died there in 1807.

18. After his term he was a magistrate in the Eure and later a *conseiller* in the Royal Court in Rouen. He died there in 1821.

19. He was also elected to the Convention, after which he returned to his business with minor excursions into politics. He died in 1851 at 96.

ship to the body from which the people, loyal to the monarchy, expected so much. The Third Estate refused to organize as a separate body, since the issue of the mode of meeting and voting had not been resolved on May 5, nor in the five weeks thereafter. Finally, on June 12, it began to verify the credentials of its members as representatives of the nation rather than as of the Third Estate. Between then and the 17th of June some parish priests joined them. The lower clergy had long been alienated from the upper clergy. The Marquis de Ferrières, a deputy of the nobility, wrote in his Mémoires: "June 1789. The Order of the Clergy, almost entirely composed of *curés*, detested equally the bishops and the nobility, and desired in secret to unite with the Third Estate. The bishops, far from trying to bring back the *curés* by services, and attempts to mingle with them, as members of the same Order, held them at a humiliating distance; always standing on episcopal haughtiness, they affected superiority, demanded deference, and had separate seats in the hall."[20]

The members of the Third Estate on June 17, with these recruits from the clergy, declared themselves the National Assembly of France. The First Estate, by a narrow majority two days later, voted to join the others in the National Assembly. The King, stubborn and uncertain, refusing to accept the situation, closed their meeting place on June 20, prompting the barred deputies to take the "Tennis Court Oath" not to separate until the Constitution was "established and affirmed upon a solid basis." Some noblemen then joined the National Assembly. The Royal Session called by the King on June 23 was unsatisfactory and threatening to the deputies. Louis XVI capitulated to the *fait accompli* on June 27 and ordered the remaining nobles and clergy to join the great majority in the National Assembly. On July 8 the united Assembly appointed a Committee on Constitutional Procedures and on the next day it assumed the name National Constituent Assembly.

The Revolution was under way. The assembling of troops indicated that a royal *coup d'état* was being prepared. Louis dismissed the still-popular Necker and other ministers on July 11, ordering Necker to leave France at once. The country, and particularly Paris, became greatly alarmed. The center of agitation in Paris

20. *Mémoires, op. cit.*, I, p. 46.

was the Palais Royal. A provisional municipal government was established on July 13. The next day—the Fourteenth—the crowds, albeit mostly of the lower middle class, entered the Revolution by the attack upon the Bastille, more to find gunpowder than to release the prisoners of whom there were only seven. Those who stormed the Bastille, writes Professor Rudé in his *The Crowd in the French Revolution*, "far from being vagrants or down-and-outs, were men of settled abode and occupation. More surprisingly perhaps, the overwhelming majority of its captors went to the Bastille under arms as enrolled members of their local units of the newly formed *milice bourgeoise*, or Parisian National Guard."[21]

The date of the tragic comedy of the Fall of the Bastille became, of course, the symbol for republican France of the downfall of arbitrary oppression and tyranny. It also signalled the important role the crowds were to play at decisive moments in the Revolution. The King responded by removing the troops from Versailles, recalling Necker, recognizing the new municipal government in Paris with Bailly as mayor, and recognizing Lafayette as commander of the new National Guard. He also accepted the red, white and blue cockade Bailly gave him. New municipal governments and local divisions of the National Guard sprang up all over France in the early summer of 1789. Then occurred the Great Fear—Normandy was one of the areas particularly affected —the outrages of the brigands, and the burning of the chateaux and abbeys with their feudal and manorial records by the frightened, land-hungry peasants.[22]

Largely as a result of this insurrectionary violence, the members of the National Constituent Assembly on the night of August 4 in an orgy of renunciation and sacrifice by the nobles, the clergy and the landowning bourgeoisie gave up practically all their feudal, manorial and ecclesiastical rights, dues, tithes and privileges, excepting that all real or land dues were to be redeemed later in a manner yet to be determined. Reforms were promised, comprising a wide program of economic, social, judicial and ecclesiastical

21. George Rudé, *The Crowd in the French Revolution* (Oxford: Oxford University Press, 1959), p. 59.
22. For the Great Fear in Normandy see Georges Lefebvre, *La Grande Peur de 1789, op. cit.*, pp. 153–4, 176, 202–4.

change. The tangible actions and the promised reforms justify Professor Gershoy in saying that "during that long night of August 4 France of the Old Regime came to an end, and a new France was born with the dawn."[23]

The Declaration of Rights of Man and the Citizen was adopted on August 27, 1789. This bourgeois instrument embodies the heart of the Revolution in terms of ideology, principles, aspirations, interests and realities. It is the philosophical and moral sanction for the institutional reorganization of France in the effort to achieve liberty, equality and fraternity, and to preserve and protect property rights. The deputies then proceeded to discuss the Constitution. A new crisis developed when Louis, after agreeing reluctantly to the August 4 decrees, hesitated to accept the Declaration of Rights, the proposal for a unicameral legislature and the suspensive veto for the King. Again, he summoned troops to Versailles. Popular leaders in Paris aroused the hungry Sections and on October 5 a mob marched to Versailles, compelling the King to sanction the decrees and to return with his family, accompanied by a delegation from the National Assembly and the National Guard, to take up residence in the Tuileries. The National Assembly followed the King on October 19.

Thomas Lindet's most important, though modest, contributions to the Revolution came during his membership in the National Assembly. As a priest he was particularly involved in the Civil Constitution of the Clergy, and his position here helps to illumine this aspect of the Revolution. In this period, too, the greatest changes came to him in his professional and personal life. Later he became an industrious and faithful member of the Convention but, like most of its members, was overshadowed by the dictatorship of the Committee of Public Safety and by the leading Jacobins. It was Robert, his brother, who was then in the center of the stage.

Thomas Lindet wrote regularly to the municipal officers in Bernay and to his brother. These letters reveal his grasp of both national and foreign affairs. They also give sharp and clear judgments of the leaders in the National Assembly. His descriptions of exciting moments in the Assembly are terse and vivid. His

23. *The French Revolution, op. cit.*, p. 123.

frequent letters to Robert, similar in tenor to those to the municipal authorities, are more informal and blunt. They helped to
familiarize Robert with the procedures and debates in the National
Assembly and with the revolutionary atmosphere of the capital.
The first letter to the municipal officers was dated August 19,
1789. Sometimes he wrote as often as twice a day. His letters are
independent, well-balanced, well-informed and detailed. There was
excellent rapport between him and his constituents. The latter,
through the municipal officers, sent him resolutions and requests.
Thomas fulfilled his duties as a conscientious and responsible
representative. It is regrettable that the records reveal little of his
personality other than what comes through in his letters and the
stand he took on vital issues.

In the National Assembly he supported the creation of the
assignats, the sale of church properties, and took an active and
affirmative part in the adoption of the Civil Constitution of the
Clergy. He was fully committed to the reformation of the Church.
Amand Montier speaks of this "worthy priest, as remarkable for
the purity of his morals as for the firmness of his attitude." He
"personified the spirit and the aspirations of those Christian
philosophers who, at the beginning of the Revolution, had the
generosity or rather the naïvete to believe in the disinterestedness
of the privileged Orders in the face of the unanimous demonstration of the will of the people. Thomas Lindet became exasperated
at the resistance of the high clergy, whose secret designs, entirely
alien to the interest of religion, he denounced . . . The sentiments
that he felt, the aspirations that he revealed, the provisions that he
formulated were not his only; his thought was the echo of the
lower clergy, which, enlightened and virtuous, renounced its
privileges wholeheartedly, gave to the Revolution the support of
its talents and the luster of its virtues, in order to insure the
triumph of the cause of the people."[24]

Legislation concerning the Church and the clergy came as early
as August 4, 1789. The decree confiscating church property was
adopted on November 2. Thomas Lindet wrote to the municipal
officers on November 6: "The reign of the clergy is no more of

24. *Correspondance, op. cit.*, pp. vii, xiii–xiv.

this world: in order to preserve too much, it has lost everything
. . ." He concluded with an unexpected observation: "It is probable
that America, which has had an abundant harvest, will supply
us . . . I do not conceal from you however that there is too much
dependence on help from America."[25]

The National Assembly established the Ecclesiastical Committee on August 20. Its fifteen members were split into three groups;
seven members were opposed to a Civil Constitution of the Clergy,
five were its lukewarm supporters, and three were advocates of
the more extreme policy of the left center. Action within the
Committee was impossible. "The Ecclesiastical Committee has
been so badly composed," wrote Thomas Lindet, "that it is difficult for it to do any useful work. It is necessary to reorganize it."[26]
As a result of general dissatisfaction with the Committee it was
reorganized on February 7, 1790, with the appointment of fifteen
additional members, all from the left wing. Nine of the original
members resigned, leaving a committee much more favorably
disposed to fundamental changes in church-state relations. Its sub-
committee on the Civil Constitution of the Clergy presented its
first draft to the National Assembly on May 29, 1790.

Thomas Lindet's revolutionary zeal mounted steadily. He wrote
to Bernay on January 10, 1790: "When it [National Assembly]
attacked the privileges of the nobility . . . it wished feudal oppression to cease, and it ceased. When it attacked the immunities of
the clergy, but respecting religion, it wished to shake off the yoke
of superstition and this yoke was knocked off. The lawyers applauded. They induced this happy revolution which shakes off
fetters forged during centuries of ignorance and barbarity by the
nobles and the ecclesiastics . . ." The next day he wrote again to
the municipal officers: ". . . I do not know what it is that the
enemies of the Constitution defend. The old order cannot be
restored; that which the Assembly introduces, even if bad, will be
better than absolute anarchy, than civil war. The defenders of the
old system would surely be the first victims: it is necessary to

25. *Ibid.*, pp. 7–10.
26. Quoted in Eric Thompson, *Popular Sovereignty and the French Constituent Assembly, 1789–1791* (Manchester: Manchester University Press,
1951), p. 125. Chapter VIII, "Church and State," is devoted to church
legislation during the National Assembly.

consent to be free, or spill one's blood to forge one's chains. The French seem to have lost their taste for slavery."[27]

A dramatic sidelight of the Revolution and an early reference to a colorful figure is given in his letter of January 22, 1790 to Robert: "My brother, our session today was very stormy . . . The district of the Cordeliers gives us from time to time proofs of enthusiasm for liberty that become alarming. Today, six hundred men took up arms to prevent the execution of a writ of arrest against Marat, printer of a journal in which he villifies everyone." In the same letter he vividly characterized the Abbé Maury, the eloquent and inflexible defender of royalty and the Church, whose "impudence and malice are the prop of a party and the fuel of the divisions that make the debates eternal." The "cursed" (*maudit*) abbé and his supporters helped prolong the debate on a finance decree for nine hours. Referring to the Negroes in the colonies in his letter of the next day to the municipal officers, he wrote: "In the eyes of reason, the slavery of Negroes is undoubtedly an anomaly, but in the eyes of this same reason, slavery ought to be abolished with precautions. The infant who does not know how to walk should be guided by leading strings."[28]

Robert Lindet, in the meantime, was not inactive politically. He was elected mayor of Bernay on February 3, 1790, under the provisions of the Decree of December 14, 1789, by 217 votes of 320 cast. His nearest competitor, M. le Danois, received only eighty-one votes. Lindet was installed on February 9. He was named as one of three Commissioners by the King in letters patent in March to take measures at once for the establishment of the Department of the Eure, in conformity with the Decree of February 26, 1790, dividing France into departments. The other two commissioners were the Duc de Bouillon and Letellier, mayor of Evreux. Five departments were to be carved out of historic Normandy. The three Commissioners took the civil oath on April 13–14. Etienne Charavay writes that Lindet revealed "rare qual-

---

27. *Correspondance, op. cit.*, pp. 43, 50. Despite his revolutionary enthusiasm it is interesting to note that Thomas Lindet was not a member of the Jacobin Club, not appearing among the 1,100 listed in its Paris membership on December 21, 1790.

28. *Ibid.*, pp. 55–58.

ities as an administrator in the delicate operations connected with
the formation and organization of the Department of the Eure."[29]
The definitive creation of the department was proclaimed on July
17, 1790. Bernay was one of six districts in the new department.
In the elections on July 1 for the district offices the active citizens
elected Robert Lindet *procureur-syndic* for the four-year term.
He resigned as mayor of Bernay. As *procureur-syndic* Lindet sat
in the district Council and in the Directory, without vote. In his
new office he was responsible for all district lawsuits and for
overseeing the application of the laws. He was thus serving a
continuing apprenticeship in public service and administration for
the important tasks that lay before him in the Convention.

The chronological and institutional history of the Revolution
has often been told and is well known. What actually transpired
on the floor of the National Assembly as reported by one of the
deputies helps to translate the events into a living story of a very
human assemblage of men confronting a rapidly-changing revolutionary situation. Thomas Lindet, for example, reported the
lively session of February 22, 1790, to his brother. The agenda
called for discussion of a decree on public tranquillity and decrees
concerning feudal rights. But these matters were sidetracked, "The
session yesterday was long and tumultuous and without result . . ."
He spoke of the *maladresse* of the president of the Assembly and
continued: "Yesterday offered a singular scene and one that revealed the mood of the opposition." It appeared that a member
of the Left, François-Pierre Blin, a doctor from Rennes, in
speaking at the tribune against a project to bestow absolute power
on the executive authority, used this forceful expression: " 'This
would authorize sending assassins out to prevent assassinations'
. . . The galleries of the Right were emptied instantly" as the
members rushed to the tribune where an "infernal clamor went
on for a long time." The well-intentioned speaker was unable to
"calm the storm," order was finally restored and the speaker censured; but the earnest Lindet remarked that this "incident had
cost France an hour and a half."

Lindet paid grudging tribute to the Abbé de Montesquiou

29. Montier, *Robert Lindet, op. cit.*, Préface de M. Etienne Charavay,
p. iii.

(François-Xavier-Marc Antoine, duc de Montesquieu-Fezensac) when he became president of the National Assembly on March 1, 1790. "L'Abbé de Montesquieu, the new president, will give activity to the Assembly and one can count on a good fortnight. Ecclesiastical privileges have no more zealous defender . . . But, pliant, adroit, insinuating, ingenious, he knows how to be guided by circumstances . . . Jealous to profit by his position, he will be ambitious to make his presidency remarkable by the quantity of its decrees."

Thomas Lindet's concern for the interests of the urban centers and for the increase of manufactures appeared in letters of April 10 and 18, 1790. In the first he wrote: "Agriculture is the beloved deity; the interests of the towns are sacrificed to it. I fear that the balance will not be maintained in a just equilibrium. Great many persons want us to be only an agricultural people; but it is not easy to bring back a patriarchal society. The excess of rural population should be employed in the manufactures in the towns." Later, he wrote that at the moment it was time lost to plead the cause of the towns because agricultural interests and the spite of the nobles and clergy were combined against the towns.

In a letter to Robert on March 20, 1790, he commented: "Count Mirabeau gave one of those great bursts of eloquence that decide questions." On April 2 he informed his brother that he was living at 343 rue Sainte-Honoré, opposite the Capucins. On May 5 he wrote a long letter on religion, the Church and the state to the municipal officers, in which he said: "He who loves his religion also loves his *patrie*. I am a priest and a citizen: the welfare of my country is no different in my eyes, than that of my religion." He went on to defend the right of the Government to supervise the administration and expenses of the Church. On May 10 he wrote to his brother: "Viscount Mirabeau took the occasion to sound the tocsin of civil war. He announced that six thousand men and six cannon had left Toulouse to support Montauban against the Bodelais. The impudent liar was confounded at once." Two days earlier he had written that the section of the Constitution on the judiciary had been completed. He remarked that this part of the Constitution had caused considerable anxiety but that he was well satisfied with the final result although he regretted greatly that a civil and criminal code could not be completed during the current Assembly.[30]

Lindet called attention to a grave matter in a letter of June 9 to the municipal officers: "One is alarmed by the likelihood of war, and by the peace among the Powers that threaten us. If one foments war it is a measure of despair and I believe one will find it hard to forgive its authors." Two days later in a letter to his brother he noted the sympathetic action of the National Assembly: "Homage rendered to the defenders of the nations: three days of mourning decreed for the death of M. Franklin." He returned to the possibilities of war and its likely dire consequences in another letter, on July 5: "We will soon have a Constitution; we have wheat; all can progress, given peace: but my opinion is that war would sweep away our wheat, our Constitution, our assignats, and our internal enemies would cause frightful calamities . . . I return to war: the enemies of the Constitution want it; they have no expedients or hopes other than war." The next day he wrote to the municipal officers elaborating his opposition to war and to the machinations of the war party. The maintenance of peace would make it possible to consolidate the Revolution; France's greatest enemies were at home and not abroad. In the recent war the French had fought for the independence of America and for the free navigation of the seas. It would be fatal to the newly-won liberties of the French to become involved in the struggle of the Powers in Europe, which he called the "war of the kings against the people." His description of the contemporary power system was shrewd and realistic. The deputy reported to his brother on July 16 that the "fête of July 14 has passed without accident; the terrors of Paris and the provinces are dispelled; everyone has returned home well satisfied."[31]

The National Assembly attended seriously to church reform in 1790. Monastic vows were prohibited by decree on February 13. The Ecclesiastical Committee submitted its proposal of reform on April 21 and the plan was taken up article by article by the National Assembly. This Civil Constitution of the Clergy was

---

30. Montier, *Correspondance*, pp. 92–3, 101, 116, 130, 138–9, 148, 155, 160.
31. *Ibid.*, pp. 179, 183–4, 201–3, 207.

adopted on July 12, 1790, and the decree requiring the clerical oath on November 27. The Papacy answered with the Papal Bull *Charitas* on April 13, 1791, and the National Assembly responded on June 9 with a decree Restricting the Publication of Papal Documents in France.

The Civil Constitution reduced the dioceses from 139 to 83, conforming to the new departments. The priests, as public officials paid by the state, were to be elected, with the departmental electors selecting the bishops and the district electors the parish priests. These would appoint their own vicars. Salaries of the higher and lower clergy were to be revised in an equitable fashion to the benefit of the lower clergy. The pope lost his "jurisdiction" but his "primacy" was recognized. Bishops were not to be confirmed by the pope.

Thomas Lindet steadily supported the ecclesiastical legislation of the National Assembly. In his letters he stated and defended his position in forceful terms, both as a reforming priest and as a practical patriot committed fully to the Revolution. How active he actually was in the debates in the Assembly is not known. In his correspondence he was severe in his judgments on the clerical opponents of the Civil Constitution, whom he bracketed with the nobles of the right and other intransigent supporters of the monarchy of the Old Regime.[32]

The King accepted the Civil Constitution on July 22. The French ambassador to Rome, Cardinal Bernis, was instructed to obtain the pope's consent. The hostile pontiff delayed his answer and finally, on November 27, the National Assembly decreed that all active priests must take an oath adhering to the Constitution of the kingdom, including, of course, the Civil Constitution. The devout king reluctantly approved this decree on December 26. Those refusing to take the oath were to lose the right to administer the sacraments and would be replaced as priests, although they would receive a pension. Seven bishops took the oath. Thomas Lindet took the oath on December 27, as one of the first clerical deputies to do so. Parish priests throughout the land divided fairly evenly in taking the oath, with some variations by regions. The newly-elected bishops were consecrated by Talleyrand, Bishop of

32. *Ibid.*, pp. 246–257.

Autun, and Gobel, Bishop of Lydda and future Bishop of Paris.

Pope Pius VI, at last, on March 11 and April 13, 1791, condemned the Civil Constitution, the abolition of tithes, the suppression of the annates, and the principles of the Revolution. The Papal Bull *Charitas* (April 13) forbade all ecclesiastics in France to take the oath; if they had already done so they were to retract within forty days from April 13. Elections of the juring bishops was declared to be "illegitimate, sacrilegious, and were and are absolutely null and void . . . The *Consecrations* of these were and are criminal, and altogether illicit, illegitimate, sacrilegious, and performed in violation of the sacred canons; and . . . we declare them . . . *suspended* from all employment of the episcopal office."[33]

Thomas Lindet, who had been elected Bishop of Evreux on February 15, 1791, was named as one whose election was nullified by the Papal Bull. He had been involved deeply and conscientiously in this crisis, particularly after he was elected bishop. The departmental archives in Evreux are full of documents on the consequences of the Civil Constitution and of Lindet's election as bishop. The pope's stand further alienated Louis XVI from the Revolution, split the Church, profoundly disturbed the faithful, drove many into counter-revolution and civil war, and made irremediable the break with Rome.

In ancient Normandy 3,519 ecclesiastics (48.27%) took the oath and 3,771 refused. In the new Department of the Eure 832 (61.58%) took it and 519 refused. In the District of Bernay 154 (58.11%) took the oath and 111 refused.[34] François de Narbonne, Bishop of Evreux from 1775 to the time of the Civil Constitution of the Clergy, refused to take the oath but continued to claim the office after Thomas Lindet was elected to succeed him.[35]

Lindet circulated a pamphlet on the taking of the oath on December 26, 1790, with another version on the 30th. In his

33. Stewart, *A Documentary Survey, op. cit.,* pp. 186–7.

34. Em. Sévestre, *Le Personnel de l'Eglise Constitutionnelle en Normandie, 1791–1795* (Paris: Auguste Picard, éd., 1925), p. 297.

35. M. A. Chassant and M.G.-E. Sauvage, *Histoire des Évêques D'Evreux* (Evreux: Louis Tavernier et Cie., 1846), pp. iii–iv; 177–179. As chaplain to the sisters of Louis XVI, Narbonne followed them into exile and died in Rome in 1792.

correspondence with his brother and the municipal authorities of Bernay he referred frequently to the Civil Constitution. The municipal officers supported his views in a communication dated December 20, which criticised a pastoral letter of Feron, the replaced non-juring Bishop of Lisieux, and its "dangerous effects." The communication called upon Lindet's parishioners to spread his views in order to "reassure those of timid conscience and enlighten those who have a too facile inclination to contribute to the error of fanaticism."[36]

Thomas Lindet in writing his brother on February 7, 1791, urged opposition to his election as bishop: "It seems to me that nothing but advantage for the new order of affairs can result if the most zealous partisans of the reform of the clergy prove in an unmistakable manner that speculations of ambition and interest have not determined their vote."[37] In the meantime the electors of the Department of the Eure assembled early in February to elect a juring bishop. The election was effected on the 15th when, after three ballots, Thomas Lindet was chosen by 238 votes to 180. M. Morsent, president of the electoral assembly, proclaimed the results and a solemn mass with music was celebrated. "All of the bells of the town were rung and a dozen cannon shots were fired," wrote a contemporary.[38] The new bishop acknowledged his election in a letter to the municipal officers on February 20: ". . . If I have the courage to accept the place which your votes have given me, I vow to you that you have put me in a position in which my regrets exceed my gratitude."[39]

Having been consecrated bishop in Paris on March 6 in the Church of the Oratoire, Lindet renewed the civil oath in the ancient Cathedral of Evreux before his local consecration and installation

---

36. Em. Sévestre, *La Vie religeuse dans les principales villes Normandes pendant la Révolution (1787–1801)*, première série-Calvados (Paris: Auguste Picard, éd., 1945), p. 397.
37. Montier, *Correspondance*, p. 265.
38. N. P. Rogue, T.B. éd., *Souvenirs et Journal d'un Bourgeois d'Evreux, 1740–1830* (Evreux: Imprimerie de A. Herissey, 1850), p. 38. See T. Bonnin, *Notes, Fragments et Documents pour servir à l'Histoire de la Ville d'Evreux, Extraite des Journaux, Memoriaux, Actes et Déliberations de l'Hôtel-de-Ville, 1623–1815* (Evreux: Imprimerie de Louis Tavernier et Cie., 1847), p. 94.
39. Montier, *Correspondance*, p. 267.

on March 27. The officers of the department, district and municipality and the National Guard under arms attended the ceremony. After vespers, a *Te Deum* was sung and there was an "illumination in the town."[40] On the same day the new bishop addressed a circular letter to the faithful, explaining the Civil Constitution of the Clergy and inviting all the priests and people to conform to the law.

The law of April 10, 1791 abolished all the parishes of Evreux and united them into one with the Cathedral. Bishop Lindet explained this on April 22 as a *Mandement* to the faithful: ". . . The circumstances of this city, its dependencies and population no longer require the number of parishes that formerly existed. The Cathedral, mother of the other churches of the city, had become sterile; it no longer had its children . . . The Cathedral, which Jesus Christ had charged to preach, to instruct, to edify and to console—deserted and abandoned—seemed condemned to inaction and silence . . . We have ardently desired the reform of abuses; we have wished to celebrate Easter with you . . . In reuniting our bodies in the same temple we hope to unite our hearts in the indissoluble bonds of love . . . Our present Mandate will be communicated to the Administrators of the Department of the Eure for its execution."[41]

The electoral assembly of Bernay district met on May 8–12, 1791, in the Church of Sainte-Croix to replace the non-juring priests in the various parishes, and that of Sainte-Croix, vacated by Thomas Lindet when he assumed the episcopacy. There were fifty-nine electors, of whom eight were from the town of Bernay. Robert Lindet, one of these, was elected president of the assembly with all but two of the fifty-nine votes. M. Lefêvre was elected to fill Thomas Lindet's place; sixty vacancies were filled; those in the tiny parishes were left vacant. The installation of the new priests was held on May 14, with the "usual pomp."[42]

The deposed Bishop de Narbonne was accused of *lèse-nation* in the late winter and early spring of 1791. He replied vigorously

40. Rogue, *op. cit.*, p. 39.

41. Archives Départmentales de l'Eure, 57 L 4, *Mandement de M. Lindet, Évêque du Département de l'Eure.*

42. Arch. Dept., de l'Eure, 11 L 10; Montier, *Robert Lindet, op. cit.*, pp. 12–13.

in pamphlets that challenged the right and authority of the secular power to determine ecclesiastical affairs, claiming that by its origin in Christ and the apostles the Church alone had jurisdiction over religious and ecclesiastical matters.[43] Narbonne circulated a thirty-six page brochure in the diocese of Evreux on June 1, including the Papal Bull *Charitas* and a five-page message from himself. He followed this on July 12 with a seventy-one page pastoral letter addressed to the "secular and regular clergy, and to all the faithful of his diocese."[44]

This pastoral letter was a long defense of the sovereign authority of the Church in spiritual and ecclesiastical matters, supported by references to the Old and New Testaments, and buttressed by historical documentation. Narbonne then interpellated Bishop Lindet, accusing him of dividing the Church and destroying its unity. "You come in whose name? Is it in the name of Jesus Christ? But he speaks only through His Church; the Church speaks with the voice of the head of the Church, whom you call anathema. You would have the Church governed by a purely secular assembly but has Jesus Christ given to civil assemblies the right to dispose of the government of His Church?" After quoting Saint Paul, Narbonne continued: "You, Monsieur, are an intruder . . . Who has placed you on His throne? The electors have arrogated to themselves the power to create priests, in spite of the opposition of the Church, to which alone belongs the right to appoint priests and establish the form by which they are to be installed. You have not entered the sheepfold by the gate."

Narbonne accused Lindet of having been consecrated wrongfully and sacrilegiously by a disqualified bishop—Talleyrand. "You do not want to be schismatic, this I know; but you are already . . . What then, my dear colleague with whom I have dwelt hitherto in such cordial unanimity? . . . For nearly twenty

43. Arch. Dep't. de l'Eure, 57 L 4. Cultes, 1791–1792. Mandements, etc., de Thomas Lindet, évêque. Brochures pour ou contre la Constitution civile.
44. Arch. Dep't. de l'Eure. 57 L 4. Lettre de Pie VI au sujet du serment de la Constitution civile adressé au Clergé et Peuple du Royaume de France et distribuée par L'Évêque François de Narbonne dans les principaux lieux de Son Diocèse 1er Juin 1791; Arch. Dep't. de l'Eure. 57 L 4. Lettre Pastorale et Ordonnance de Mgr. L'Évêque d'Evreux (François de Narbonne), 12 juillet, 1791.

years we walked together in concert in the house of God." He
appealed to Lindet, both tenderly and logically, to expiate his
wrong. He then forbade the priests and the faithful to accept
Lindet as their bishop and declared him to be suspended from all
his sacerdotal functions. There was a final seven-page letter from
Narbonne to the juring priests of his former diocese who had
subsequently retracted their oath, dated from Rome, February 15,
1792.[45]

Abbé Baston, former professor of the Sorbonne, canon of Rouen
and an old friend of Thomas Lindet, refused to take the civil oath
and exiled himself in England. He and Lindet engaged in a vigorous exchange of polemics which enjoyed a "limited fame."[46] In
his *Mémoires* the Abbé quotes one of Lindet's letters, concluding
with his own comment: "This piece is not well written, nor well
thought out; but it is curious."[47]

Louis XVI in the meantime had been planning since December
1790 to escape from France in order to head the foreign intervention he hoped would restore the monarchy to its traditional power
and authority. Finally, on June 20, 1791, the King and the royal
family fled Paris, only to be apprehended and arrested at Varennes
the following day. On his humiliating return to Paris on the 24th
he was virtually suspended by the National Assembly and made
a prisoner of state until he should approve and accept the revised
Constitution. Thomas Lindet wrote to his brother on June 22:
"Will Louis XVI remount the throne from which he has descended?
Will he have a successor? . . . Will not France become a Republic?
When will this happen? How do we bring it off? . . ." On the
same day he wrote to the municipal officers: "The King has been
arrested at Varennes; the inhabitants have saved France from the
extremities of civil and foreign war."[48] Aulard comments that "the

45. Arch. Dep't. de l'Eure. 57 L 4. Lettre de Monseigneur L'Évêque
d'Evreux aux Curés de son diocèse, qui se sont retractés de leur serment,
qui les releve de la suspense qu'ils ont encourue et les rétablit dans leurs
fonctions.
46. Abbé Augustin Sicard, *Le Clergé de France pendant la Révolution*
(Paris: Librairie Lecoffre, 1927), II, pp. 292-3.
47. *Mémoires de l'Abbé Baston-Chanoine de Rouen.* éd. L'Abbé Julien
Loth et Ch. Verger (Paris: Alphonse Picard et Fils, 1899), II, pp. 52-3.
48. Montier, *Correspondance*, p. 283.

letters of Thomas Lindet at the time are those of a Republican."[49] The "republican" wrote to his brother on July 18: "Hatred of the King makes one desire the abolition of royalty; fear of disorder may reconcile us to royalty, and perhaps with the King." In a letter two days previously he had stated impersonally: "The Jacobin Club is becoming schismatic" over the question of the status of the King after Varennes. On the 12th he described vividly the enthusiastic "pantheonization of Voltaire in Paris, which had begun on July 10.[50]

Thomas Lindet was bitterly critical of the Government and the trend of events on August 1, 1791: "My brother, I must confess that we are badly served. Several of our ministers are evidently knaves; our Military Committee is tripartite of aristocrats, imbeciles and rogues. Our Committee of Finance is made up of rascals who speculate in order to drain the last penny from France, and who have conceived all the tricks possible to retard and prevent the production of assignats of small denomination . . . Will we have war? many desire it . . . It is unfortunate that a new legislative body has not replaced us; it would display more activity, more unity, more force, but I believe that, just as the Revolution has been made without design, without contrivance, without concord, so the war will be decided by the force of circumstances, by the irresistible mass of the general will. The fate of the battles, too, will depend on opinion."

These acute and troubled observations by a weary and discouraged deputy were continued in a letter on August 15: "Send us incorruptible successors. We leave to them a king, surrounded by suspected ministers; we transmit to them false accounts of the state of our frontiers, of our armies, of our manufactures, of the state of our enemies . . . We leave to them our complicated finances . . . We leave to them an ignorant or inactive administrative corps as well as corrupt courts. We leave to them little force, few means." Ten days later he wrote to his brother: "The Thourets, Barnaves, Andres, Duports and above all the Lameths have earned the incontestable right to public execration."

49. A. Aulard, *Histoire Politique de la Révolution Française* (Paris: Librairie Armand Colin, 1905), p. 121 n.
50. Montier, *Correspondance*, pp. 296–7, 299, 301.

This last-named moderate bourgeois group, fearful of mass action, desirous of protecting its property rights and taking an anti-republican line in favor of the restoration of the suspected king, was advocating a conservative revision of the Constitution. With others they left the Jacobin Club during the crisis and established the Feuillants. Thomas Lindet commented on this in a letter on December 20, from Evreux to Robert, now in Paris as a member of the Legislative Assembly: "The division of Feuillants and the Jacobins at the end of the Assembly was fatal; it will be no less so for you." On the 28th he again wrote: "Are the Carras, Marats, Desmoulins sleeping? It is up to them to carry terror to the despots of Europe." Prior to this and near the adjournment of the National Assembly Louis XVI appeared before the Assembly on September 14 and formally accepted the revised Constitution. Thomas Lindet reported the event to his brother: "It is thus appropriate that the first functionary reconcile himself with his people and resume an air of dignity."[51]

The last session of the National Assembly was held on September 30 and on the following day the newly-elected Legislative Assembly took over for its prescribed two-year term. The new Constitution stressed separation of powers between the legislature, king and elected judges. The Legislative Assembly had the exclusive power to initiate and make the laws and could not be dissolved by the King. The latter had a suspensive veto over ordinary legislation. The deputies had full parliamentary immunity. The legislature assessed the taxes and controlled public expenditures. Its previous consent was necessary for the declaration of war and the ratification of treaties. Diplomacy was under its jurisdiction and it directed the ministry. The king's executive powers were carefully restricted by the legislature.

Thomas Lindet joyfully announced the termination of the National Assembly: "My brother, finally we are free . . . Our final session was brilliant. The king gave a very constitutional and much applauded speech . . . The ecclesiastical war is not over; the irreconciliable clergy, fatally wounded, will try to carry us along with it to its downfall."[52]

51. *Ibid.*, pp. 303–4, 308–310, 317, 327.
52. *Ibid.*, p. 321.

In his role of bishop, Thomas Lindet sent a fifteen-page mandate to the faithful of his diocese on September 15, the day after the King had accepted the Constitution: "Our very dear Brothers, the day desired by all of France has finally arrived. Your representatives have fulfilled the honorable mission you gave to them. A new government founded on justice, liberty and equality will raise up again the French, bowed down for so long under the yoke of despotism . . . An austere regime is substituted for the old wastefulness of the public treasury . . . We will no longer listen to the sham zealots of the altar cry out about what one has done to religion, because it no longer gives them food for intrigue, for ambition, for rapacity, and for the scandalous luxury of servile slaves of the Court, of vile adulators and odius complices of the vices of the courtiers.

"The ministers of the church no longer invoke the influence and power of the great in order to advance in the church. They will think of the need they will have of talent, of enlightenment, and of virtue; and the judgment of the people will almost without fail remove all those who do not offer these guarantees of success for their ministry. Faith, the gift of heaven, will not be taken away from France. You will not be less Christian because your pontiff and priests are bound to be more virtuous . . . This day will be forever memorable in the annals of France, this day which terminates the revolution, which binds the monarch and the nation by the most sacred pledges . . . Frenchmen, you were vicious when you were slaves; you are now free and will become virtuous . . . One cannot be faithful to the law of God when one is unfaithful to the law of his land, when this law is not in evident opposition to the divine law."[53]

On his return to Evreux from the National Assembly Bishop Lindet issued a thirty-three page printed circular letter to the clergy of his diocese on October 2 and a sixteen-page letter to the religious of the monasteries on October 25. His constituents honored him and Buzot for their services in the National Assembly with a *grande fête* on October 30, arranged by the Society of the Friends of the Constitution and the public authorities of Evreux. An eighty-four year old war veteran presented Lindet with a sash

53. Arch. Dep't. de l'Eure, 57 L 4.

in the three revolutionary colors, on which was the inscription:
A Thomas Lindet, la garde nationale d'Evreux reconnaissante.
Duvaucel, the mayor, then bestowed on him the civic crown.[54]

In his capacity as bishop, Thomas Lindet issued a lengthy
Pastoral Instruction on March 16, 1792, prompted by local civic
and religious disturbances. "We speak to you with the charity of
the Christian and with the firmness of the citizen who has vowed
to uphold the laws." He called attention to the alarms sounded by
trouble-makers, to an impending scarcity of food, high taxes on
grain, failure of the municipal officers to enforce the law, the
inability of the national guard to put down disorder and brigandage, the disappearance of commodities, the enormous expenses
of government, hunger in spite of abundant harvests, disturbed
markets, and the indifference of neighboring regions to the needs
of a suffering one. He spoke as a bourgeois when he said: "With
liberty, [but] without property there is no longer a society; without
fidelity in maintaining them both the social pact cannot exist."

Lindet proceeded to defend the constitutional Church and juring
clergy against their calumniators, including the pope. He concluded
this passage: "In the name of reason and the Gospel, we preach
union and concord, submission to the laws, respect for the lawful
authorities, fidelity to your vows, exactitude in fulfilling the duties
of the citizen . . . We preach the love of your brother, indulgence
of your enemies, justice towards all . . . We preach liberty under
the reign of law . . . We preach submission to the law, because it
is made by you and for you."[55] Later that year, on August 20, in
a letter to his brother he made an unexpected observation for a
priest and a bishop: "Theism and Protestantism have greater con-
nections with republicanism [than Catholicism]. Catholicism has
always been attached to the monarchy."[56]

After his election to the Convention in 1792, Thomas Lindet
circulated another pamphlet in which he expressed his desire to
resign the episcopacy since he could not give his full time to it.
Among other items in this brochure he gave his ideas on the

54. Chassant et Sauvage, *op. cit.*, p. 148.
55. *Instruction Pastorale* de Monsieur Lindet, Evêque du Département de
l'Eure à l'occasion des troubles civils et religieux (Evreux: L'Imprimerie
de J.J.L.L. Ancelle, 1792), 54 pages.
56. Montier, *Correspondance*, p. 375.

celibacy of the clergy. First, he called attention to the misery of the people and said that the Convention was concerning itself to find the severe measures necessary to suppress the speculators and other public enemies responsible for the shortage of grain, and also to get grain from abroad. He called the scarcity a false and artificial one. He calmed those who feared the predominant power of Paris at the expense of the rights and liberties of all the French: "Brothers and Citizens, one calumniates Paris: she does not wish to, and she cannot, dominate the Departments. Your brothers in Paris love equality, they desire the Republic, they wish neither kings nor dictators, nor Tribunes, nor Triumvirs, they want no more tyrants." He turned to religion: "Religion consoled the enslaved French, it brings happiness to the free French. Its ministers, jealous of the confidence of an enlightened people, combat all superstitions and will reform all bizarre practices. They will preserve only those institutions that have a moral purpose; religious fetes will take on a national color; one will not trouble any more to speak to the French of the walls of Jericho, of the flight from Egypt, the exploits of Samson . . . One will speak of the ruins of the Bastille, of the destruction of tyrants, of the reign of liberty, the exploits of heroes of the republic, and the mysteries will be celebrated in the language of the people."

After this union of religion with civic virtue and pride, he continued: "It is necessary to disengage the celestial doctrine of Jesus Christ from the theological opinions which only serve to obscure; it is necessary to recall the sublime virtues of Christianity, and abandon the practices of the monks and anchorites; we must conform to the laws of the Republic . . . Public opinion outlaws the celibacy of the priests. It is not commanded by the author of the religion, nor by the apostles . . . It has become the object of a multitude of regulations and scandals . . . Is it necessary to maintain such an institution? . . . When the author of nature has ordained that man and woman should unite and multiply, who can forbid it? . . . It is time that priests return to the law which governs the human race and all of nature."[57]

Thomas Lindet had come a long way in his thinking from the

---

57. Robert-Thomas Lindet, Evêque du Département de l'Eure, aux Citoyens du même Département (Paris: Chez Boulard, 1792), 30 pages.

days of his humble parish priesthood prior to the Revolution. Events had accelerated these processes of thought and conviction and the Revolution had forced issues that otherwise would never have been faced and ultimately resolved. He was honest enough to resolve them and in the process the priest-bishop was metamorphized into the virtuous republican patriot above all else. A symbol of this was his marriage.

Bishop Lindet sent a letter to the authorities of Evreux on February 19, 1793, announcing that he had "overcome all prejudices and had contracted marriage in the month of December 1792."[58] After the civil ceremony Lindet and his bride—apparently his housekeeper—had the religious rites performed by the Abbé Claude Bernard in the Church of Sainte-Marguerite in Paris. In announcing the event to the municipality of Bernay, he wrote: "I have practiced all the civic and religious virtues. One great example remained for me to perform, namely, to rise above superstitious prejudices; I have done this and I have chosen a companion with whom I shall give the example of domestic virtues."[59]

Le Moniteur reported the event but dated it in November. In the Convention on Saturday, November 24, Manuel took the tribune to declare: "I announce to the Convention, whose duty it is to form the public morale, that Lindet, Bishop of Evreux, is married. I request an honorable mention." Prieur followed: "I ask the order of the day since it is not necessary to acknowledge that which is only the duty of the citizen."[60] Under the news items for France and Paris, with the date line of November 27, *Le Moniteur*, after giving a communication from the Executive Council to the Pope, reported: "Citizen Lindet, bishop of Evreux, ex-deputy of the Constituent Assembly, and member of the National Convention, was married in Paris. The vicar of the parish Sainte-Marguerite, himself a father, gave him the nuptial benediction after the Catholic rite. For an added benefit, the *patrie* and society are indebted for this unexpected example of a person of

58. Chassant et Sauvage, *op. cit.*, p. 185; cf. Bonin, *op. cit.*, p. 101; Rogue, *op. cit.*, p. 56.
59. Pierre de la Gorce, *Histoire Religieuse de la Révolution Française* (Paris: Librairie Plon, 1909–   ), III (1918), pp. 46–7.
60. *Moniteur* (Réimpression), XIV, p. 560.

upright reputation and amiable character who enjoys the esteem of all who know him."[61] The marriage was also reported at the Jacobin Club in Paris on November 21: "A citizen announced that not only priests were marrying but that bishops, too, were also paying the debt of nature. 'I learn,' he announced to the society, 'that the Bishop of Evreux is married.' (applause)."[62]

Bishop Lindet publicly resigned his episcopal office in early 1793 at the tribune of the Convention. The evolution of the religious and political thought of this intelligent, sensitive and honest ecclesiastic was representative of others under the circumstances of a fundamental revolution against the institutions and sanctions of the Old Regime. That he had not forfeited the confidence and trust of his constituents is attested to by the fact that he was elected to the Council of Elders in 1795 from the Department of the Eure, at the conclusion of his membership in the Convention.

61. *Ibid.*, p. 570.
62. F.-A. Aulard, *La Société des Jacobins. Recueil de Documents pour l'Histoire Du Club des Jacobins de Paris* (Paris: Librairie Jouast, 1892), p. 504.

CHAPTER THREE

Robert Lindet—Legislator

ROBERT LINDET WAS ELECTED to the Legislative Assembly in August, 1791. He had by then served a worthy and practical apprenticeship in the Revolution for usefulness at the national level. In his professional career, as early as 1776 while *procureur du roi* in Bernay, he had become familiar with fiscal and financial matters, providing him a solid knowledge of local administration in the Old Regime. He had been the principal editor of the *cahier* of Bernay as a member of the Third Estate there, and was a member of the General Assembly of the Three Orders in Evreux in 1789. He had been mayor of Bernay in 1790, was one of three Commissioners appointed by the King in March 1790 to establish the new Department of the Eure, and had been elected in July as *procureur-syndic* of the district of Bernay, one of the six districts of the new department. In the fulfillment of these several responsibilities he had won the respect and confidence of his fellow citizens. In addition, his political education had been furthered at the national level during the National Assembly by his brother Thomas, who had kept him up to date in his frequent and illuminating accounts of deliberations in the Assembly, supplemented by his regular reports to the local authorities.

The electoral assembly of the Department of the Eure met on August 20, 1791, in the Cathedral of Evreux to elect delegates to the new Legislative Assembly. Robert Lindet was one of the electors. The sessions, lasting to September 6, were opened by a Mass in which the Supreme Being was implored to fill the hearts of the electors with the "spirit of wisdom and truth and inspire their elections with zeal for the prosperity of the State and the fulfillment of the Constitution." Robert Lindet was chosen president of the Assembly and was the first deputy elected, by a vote of 325 of the 545 voting. Ten others, and four alternates were subsequently elected.

Robert Lindet resigned as *procureur-syndic* on October 15, when he went to Paris to assume his new duties. Thomas had found quarters for him in the apartment of M. Colon, a surgeon, at 339, rue Saint-Honoré, where two other deputies were lodged. This was a neighborhood in the very heart of Paris, frequented by deputies because of its nearness to the Legislative Assembly.

What kind of person was this new legislator and future member of the famous Committee of Public Safety, as he crossed the threshold into national public service? Amand Montier finds he was a person of calm reflection and firm decision, a sagacious Norman with a great capacity for work, absolutely devoted to the public cause, simple and modest—and a provincial who remained a provincial.[1] Etienne Charavay, in his preface to Montier's biography, describes Lindet as one who was "wise and prudent, who did not give way to the caprices of opinion or to the violence of passion, but who made up his mind by the principles of sound reason." He speaks of "rare qualities of administration in the delicate operations associated with the establishment of the Department of the Eure." Boivin-Champeaux paints a word picture: "His countenance was intellectual and his features were endowed with an extreme mobility. A smile was habitually on his lips, but a trace of irony sharpened his glance. All was so well arranged that those who met him for the first time were not sure whether they had received a caress or a cut . . . So far as power was concerned he feared only its pomp; he liked only work and responsibility. Here was a man, less of politics than administration . . . His reports, oftentimes too long, sparkled less by their elegance and embossing than by their clarity."[2] Lindet lacked a strong speaking

1. *Robert Lindet, op. cit.,* p. 16.
2. L. Boivin-Champeaux, *Notices Historiques sur la Révolution dans le Département de l'Eure* (Evreux: de l'Imprimerie Auguste Herissey, 1868), pp. 160–1.

voice and often had Cambon speak for him during the Legislative Assembly.

That body met for the first time on October 1, 1791. By its "self-denying" ordinance, members of the National Assembly had declared themselves ineligible for election to the new group, depriving it of the talents and legislative experience of some of the able men who had constituted the first assembly. The members of the new assembly were drawn largely from the middle bourgeoisie of lawyers, other professions, and publicists. Norman Hampson comments that two-thirds of the deputies came from posts in local governments or were judges and magistrates in the newly-established courts.[3]

The 745 members divided themselves into three political groupings: the right with 264 members, the left with 136, and the remaining 345 in the center, as independents. Most members, in the beginning, were committed to the constitutional monarchy and hoped to make the constitution work. The members of the right were inscribed in the Feuillants.[4] They were generally favorable to the constitutional monarchy, were opposed both to the Old Regime and to republicanism, and were devoted to the primacy of the bourgeoisie. They lacked outstanding leaders within the Legislative Assembly. Their real leaders were outside—Barnave, Lameth, Duport and Lafayette. The latter played a role of intrigue and duplicity during this period and became distrusted alike by the Feuillants and the King. The Lafayettists frequented the salon of Madame de Staël. Jacques Godechot goes so far as to call Lafayette a "royalist and hostile to the Republic."[5]

The Jacobins and the Cordeliers comprised the Left. Their dominant leaders in the early months of the Legislative Assembly were the Girondins, or Brissotins, whose leaders were Brissot, Vergniaud and Condorcet. Many of these came from the Gironde and were moderate bourgeois republicans who represented the interests of the provincials. Their attitude towards the *sans-culottes* was condescending. They consorted with shipowners, bankers,

3. Norman Hampson, *A Social History of the French Revolution* (London: Routledge and Kegan Paul, 1963), p. 132.

4. *Supra*, p. 48.

5. Jacques Godechot, *La Contre-Révolution. Doctrine et Action, 1789–1804* (Paris: Presses Universitaires de France, 1961), p. 179.

great merchants and entrepreneurs, and represented the economic "liberalism" of the wealthy. They not only frequented the stimulating salon of Madame Roland, able and ambitious wife of one of their less able leaders, but also that of Madame Dodun, the wealthy widow of a farmer-general, in the fashionable Place Vendôme. Brissot, a Paris journalist, was a political opportunist. Vergniaud, a lawyer and son of a merchant, was their eloquent mouthpiece in the Assembly; he was fastidious, indolent and indecisive. Condorcet, the "philosopher of the Republic," a mathematician and friend of Voltaire, d'Alembert, and Turgot, was a highly-respected person of great integrity and idealism. In foreign affairs they were steadfastly the "war Party," hoping for a preventive war, and wishing to use it, as Lefebvre puts it, as a political manoeuvre, as a war of propaganda and ideology.

Rising leaders of the Left, other than the Girondins, were Couthon, Robespierre, Danton, and Marat, who generally represented the interests of the capital, and were radical, popular republicans. It is not certain where Robert Lindet belonged at first. "Constitutional monarchist," writes Charavay, "like the majority of his colleagues, he was converted gradually to the republican idea under the influence of developments."[6] Certainly he had been influenced in this direction by Thomas Lindet's experiences in the National Assembly. In the Convention he was to sit with the Montagnards. The writer can find no evidence for Albert Soboul's contention that Lindet sat on the extreme left in the Legislative Assembly along with Couthon and Carnot.[7]

The major initial task of the Legislative Assembly and the King was to govern France under the new Constitution and thus to consolidate the revolution. Paramount problems were: the émigrés and counter-revolution, the refractory clergy, finances and the economy, the depreciation of the *assignats* and inflation, the German princes and the threat of war, and the uncertain fidelity of the King to the Constitution. This last fact overshadowed the life of

6. Montier, *Robert Lindet, op. cit.*, iii.
7. Albert Soboul, *La Révolution française, 1789–1799* (Paris: Editions Sociales, 1951), p. 163: "On the extreme left, were certain supporters of universal suffrage, such as Robert Lindet, Couthon, Carnot. Three deputies, united in close intimacy, Basire, Chabot, Merlin de Thionville, formed the Cordelier trio." This is a strange classification, too, for Carnot.

the Legislative Assembly. After Varennes, none but the die-hard royalists trusted the monarch. Suspicion of him as the principal counter-revolutionary conspirator mounted steadily. In this atmosphere of fear, distrust, suspicion, rumour, and panic the Legislative Assembly was fated to labor and die before the end of its first year. History indisputably proves the complicity of the King and Queen with the émigrés and foreign enemies of the Revolution.

The short life of the Legislative Assembly was turbulent. The treason of the King, the foreign invasion, the Brunswick Manifesto, economic distress, social disorder, and the intervention of the Paris Commune, Sections and crowds, produced the "revolution" of August 9–10 and the September Massacres. The latter gave the *coup de grace* to the Legislative Assembly, caused the suspension of the King, and the calling of the Convention, elected by universal male suffrage.

These crises and events obstructed and prevented constructive work by the deputies. The important "Report on the General Organization of Education," for instance, was held over for implementation by the Convention. This document, composed under the chairmanship of Condorcet, laid down many of the principles for modern education in the secular state—free, compulsory, and universal.

Robert Lindet's role in the Legislative Assembly was modest. He was a member of the Committee of Liquidation and a "most efficient" member of the Finance Committee.[8] J. N. Davy, an historian of the Eure, describes Lindet's conduct in the Legislative Assembly in commendatory terms: Lindet remained outside the "combinations and intrigues" of the groups. "With an alert and keen mind . . . firm friend of the Revolution, resolute in his devotion to France and to liberty, too honest to put these in the scales with the interests of a sect, caste, or throne, with a great talent for administration, a consummate man of affairs, Robert Lindet sought more to be useful to the public welfare than to shine personally in the Assembly which was charged to put into practice the new institutions. For another reason, he had a voice too weak to use the tribune to good advantage in a large assembly . . . Full of

8. H. Morse Stephens, *A History of the French Revolution* (New York: Charles Scribners' and Sons, 1905), p. 305.

disdain for the pretexts of the ambitious and scorn for the plots of the intriguers, Robert Lindet remained immovable in the conviction that only the force of patriotism could save France and the revolution from the fate which the King and the European coalition planned for them."[9]

Montier reports that Robert Lindet's experience in the Legislative Assembly was one of "observation, study, and reflection," and that the "political experience acquired in the *ombre* of committees," prepared him for his later service in the Convention.[10] Robert kept in close touch with affairs in the Eure through regular letters from his brother Thomas, busy with his duties as juring Bishop of Evreux. Sometimes these were daily letters but generally they were written every week or ten days and were dated from either Bernay or Evreux. They contained detailed reports on events in the department and were interlarded with acute, patriotic and republican observations. They also commented shrewdly on events in Paris. Thomas referred frequently to letters from his brother. Quite likely, Robert advised Thomas in matters having to do with the administration of his episcopal office.[11]

War was on the agenda from the beginning. The Girondins desired a war of defense and of ideology, a war against tyrants, that would "unmask the King and his suspected treason," and would increase their popularity and power. The military clique wished a successful war to strengthen the monarchy and purge the Jacobins. Louis XVI desired a short, interventionary war to restore his traditional power and authority. The Feuillants opposed the war. Robespierre was the one radical leader who, almost single-handedly at first, opposed war. He wanted primarily to consolidate the Revolution. Feeling that the French armies were poorly prepared, he feared that war would strengthen the executive, and he feared, too, the possibility of a dictatorship.

Louis XVI, in March 1792, under strong pressure, accepted the resignation of the Feuillant ministers and appointed a new ministry committed to the war policy. The minister of foreign

9. J. N. Davy, *Les Conventionnels de l'Eure: Buzot, Duroy, Lindet* (2 vols., Evreux: De l'Imprimerie de Ernest Quettier, 1876), pp. 345-7.

10. *Robert Lindet, op. cit.*, p. 35.

11. Montier, *Correspondance, op. cit.*, pp. 322–378.

affairs was Dumouriez, a veteran of the Seven Years' War and an adventurer. Roland, Clavière, and Servan were other leading ministers. The Legislative Assembly declared war on Austria on April 20th, with a statement renouncing a war of conquest. Prussia, coming to the defense of Austria, declared war on France on May 1. It was quickly apparent that the French armies were in no condition to fight. They suffered immediate reverses at the hands of the allies.

Living conditions in the spring and summer of 1792 aggravated the crisis in foreign affairs. The assignats fell forty-one percent in August and there was serious inflation. There was a rise in prices, grain was being hoarded, food speculation was rife, bread was scarce, granaries were sacked, and there were widespread food riots. Silk factories in Tours had been closed and in Lyons, 30,000 silk weavers were out of work. The agrarian law was proposed in some quarters. The preponderance of young people in France, a great many of whom were unemployed, made them the "most explosive" group, because they were both young and unemployed.[12] In the Department of the Eure there were riots and armed uprisings because of the economic distress. Evreux was threatened and Bernay was asked by the Directors of the Department to furnish National Guards to help quell the disorders. The insurrection was quickly suppressed.[13] The selfishness, hoarding, and speculations of the landowners and middlemen prompted Thomas Lindet to write on May 16, 1792: "The aristocracy of the rich is as imperious, as ignorant, and as vexatious, as that of the nobles."[14]

The summer of 1792 was tense and critical. The oft-told narrative of events through the September Massacres need not be repeated in detail. There were ministerial changes made under pressure, threats by Lafayette to intervene with military force, mass demonstrations and mob action in Paris, the suspension of

12. Jacques Godechot, *Les Révolutions, 1770–1799* (Paris: Presses Universitaires de France, 1963), p. 86. "France especially, was predominated by youth in 1789; only 24% of its population exceeded forty years, while 40% were between twenty and forty, and 36% under twenty."
13. F. Malebranche, *Bernay pendant l'Insurrection de Mars, 1792* (Bernay: Veuve A. Lefevre, Imprimeur, 1873), p. 5.
14. Aulard, *Histoire Politique, op. cit.,* p. 453 n.

Pétion and Manuel as mayor and *procureur*, the threat of actual invasion, the unruly *fédérés* in Paris for the Fête de la Fédération, the Brunswick Manifesto of July 25, the call for volunteers, anti-palace activities of the Sections under new leaders, the distribution of pikes to unarmed citizens, and agitation by the working men's Sections, supported by some national guardsmen, to depose the King. This turbulence and violence reached a climax on August 9–10 and ran unchecked through the September Massacres.

The tocsin rang at midnight on the 9th, and the *fédérés,* armed by the insurrectionists, national guardsmen, passive citizens, and radicals of the Quinze-Vingts—working men's Section of the Faubourg Saint-Antoine—marched on the Tuileries where the Swiss Guards, a small contingent of loyal national guardsmen and a few noblemen defended the royal family. In the meantime, twenty-eight of the Sections sent delegations to the Hôtel de Ville, where the Commune was in session. During the night they ousted the Commune, arrested Mandat and appointed Santerre in his place as commander-in-chief of the National Guard. Early in the morning of the 10th the King and the royal family fled the Tuileries and took refuge in the Assembly. The palace was invaded and its defenders were slaughtered. The next day the terrified and paralyzed Assembly authorized the municipalities to arrest suspects. The revolutionary Commune took over in Paris and forced the Legislative Assembly to agree to its terms, including the suspension of the King until the convocation of the Convention. The King was turned over to the Commune, which imprisoned him and the royal family. "It was the Brunswick Manifesto," writes Professor Godechot, which "instigated August 10 and the overthrow of the throne." Lefebvre agrees that "August 10 was the reply to the Brunswick Manifesto and as such appeared to be a national revolution."[15] The municipal officers of Evreux promptly, on August 11, sent the approbation of the city to the events of the 10th to Robert Lindet, in an address prepared by Thomas Lindet. Robert read it to the Legislative Assembly to a round of applause.[16]

---

15. Godechot, *La Contre-Révolution, op. cit.,* p. 177; Georges Lefebvre, *La Révolution Française: La Chute du Roi* (Paris: Centre de Documentation Universitaire, 1940), p. 215.

16. Montier, *Robert Lindet, op. cit.,* pp. 29–30.

A provisional Executive Council was appointed to replace the King and his ministers as the executive authority. The six new ministers named included the three Girondin ministers, Roland, Clavière, and Servan, restored to their former posts, the mathematician Monge as minister of the navy, Lebrun, a journalist, minister of foreign affairs, and Danton, minister of justice. The latter, the only non-Girondin in the group, was virtually the head and master of the ministry.[17]

The struggle for power between the Assembly, Commune, and the ministry raged for the next six weeks, complicated by the new self-constituted local authorities with their own purges. A popular decree of August 14 offered the land of émigrés for sale in small plots to be distributed for an annual rent, along with a division of lands hitherto held in common. Stringent measures were levelled against the non-juring priests and on August 26 the Legislative Assembly decreed that those not taking the oath within fifteen days would either leave France or be deported. Subsequently, the legislators voted to entrust the register of births, marriages, and deaths to the civil authorities of each municipality, and authorized divorce.

Under pressure from the Commune, the Legislative Assembly decreed, on August 17, the formation of an extraordinary tribunal to try all conspirators, without appeal from its decisions. Robert Lindet opposed its establishment.[18] The guillotine was set up in the Place du Carrousel. Lafayette threatened to march on Paris with his Army of the Ardennes but, deserted by his troops, went over to the Austrians on August 19, who responded by imprisoning him. The Prussians invaded France on August 19 and on the 23rd captured Longwy, a frontier fortress.

Tensions and fear mounted in Paris and throughout the country. A great funeral demonstration for the revolutionary victims of August 10 was held in Paris on the 23rd. The Commune voted a fresh levy of 30,000, to be armed and equipped for the front. Roland and Servan proposed the removal of the Government to

17. Alphonse Aulard, *Études et Leçons sur la Révolution Française* (Quatrième série, 2me éd., Paris: Felix Alcan, 1908), Ch. VII, "Danton et la révolution du 10 aout 1792."

18. Montier, *Robert Lindet, op. cit.,* p. 32.

Tours or Blois but Danton thundered against this "craven proposal." It was decreed on August 28 to send commissioners from the Legislative Assembly to the departments, to aid recruitment, requisition supplies, and to dismiss lukewarm officials. The commissioners were given the right to make domiciliary visits and power to confiscate arms; suspects were to be arrested—and soon the prisons were full. Terrifying news arrived that Verdun was besieged—if it fell, the road to Paris would be open—and it surrendered on September 2. The Assembly and Commune united in a call for volunteers and those responding prepared to march to the front. On September 4 the Executive Council ordered requisition and price controls for grain and fodder to supply the army.

Mob massacres of the imprisoned suspects began on September 2, inflamed by passionate resolutions in several Sections and abetted by the new Watch Committee of the Commune. There were no trials and the massacres continued for four days. The slaughter spread to the terrified departments. Neither the Legislative Assembly nor the Commune took serious steps to intervene. Thomas Lindet had written to his brother from Evreux on August 20: "The Revolution is leading us far. Beware of the agrarian law."[19]

Robert Lindet's part in the events of August and September is unknown. A year later he said: "No force, no human power could resist the impetuosity of this terrible movement which seemed to be ordered by the safety of the *patrie*, and thus was, in the eyes of great numbers, but the impartial application of the principle of natural rights."[20] Alarmed by the military peril in August, he apparently wished to volunteer for service at the front. Thomas, to whom he expressed his patriotic intention, wrote on August 30: "What is this you propose to me! On the contrary, I hope the electors of the Eure will keep you in Paris. That post will be no less perilous than the frontier."[21]

During these agitated days the elections to the Convention were held. The political and emotional climate was not conducive to

19. Aulard, *Histoire Politique, op. cit.*, p. 259 n; Montier, *Correspondance*, p. 370.
20. Montier, *Robert Lindet, op. cit.*, p. 33.
21. Montier, *Correspondance*, p. 374.

calm and judicious voting. The Legislative Assembly expressed the hope on September 4 that its successor would abolish the monarchy, and the newly-elected deputies from Paris were given a mandate to that effect. In the nation-wide elections only 700,000 of 7,000,000 qualified voters actually voted. Voting in Paris and ten other departments was verbal. In Paris the Commune used terroristic methods to keep royalist sympathizers from the polls, and only sympathizers of the Commune were elected, including Marat, Danton, and Robespierre. The Girondins were snowed under in Paris but were returned in great numbers elsewhere. During this period heavy rains had impeded the march of the allied armies. Brunswick advanced, however, on Valmy and prepared to attack on September 20. The French, surprisingly, held firm and rain ended the fighting; the outcome was indecisive but Brunswick retreated.

An alarming episode happened in the Eure in early September, having a bearing on the elections of its deputies to the Convention. The Executive Council in Paris had named thirty special commissioners on August 29 to press "the extraordinary requisition of men in the sixteen departments surrounding the capital." Two of these, Momoro and Dufour, were sent to the Calvados and the Eure. Antoine-François-Momoro (1763–1794), a printer and engraver in Paris, was one of the founders of the Cordeliers and one of its most influential leaders. The two commissioners issued a declaration of rights, written and signed by Momoro, which included the suggestion of a future agrarian law. "The Normans," writes Aulard, "were greatly agitated by this menace of an agrarian law." In Bernay there was a "popular rising" against the two commissioners, and the citizens threatened to "break their necks and carry their heads to the borders [of the department]." The municipality arrested the commissioners on September 8 and brought them before the electoral assembly, where Buzot, its president, abjured Momoro to "behave with circumspection and limit himself exclusively to the object of his mission."[22] Buzot then calmed the feelings of his co-citizens and the two commissioners left Bernay without further trouble. The incident, which was widely publicised in France, so disturbed the Electoral Assembly of the

22. Aulard, *Histoire Politique, op. cit.*, pp. 260–1.

Eure, then in session, that it charged the "deputies it had elected and those it would yet elect to respect the rights of man and the citizen, as well as the rights of property, and never deviate from these principles . . . under penalty of ignominy."[23]

The Electoral Assembly of the Department of the Eure met in Bernay from September 2–15, in the Benedictine Church, and was opened by a Mass administered by Bishop Lindet. Buzot, its president, was the first deputy elected to the Convention with 409 votes of the 584 persons voting.[24] Thomas Lindet was the second elected, on September 4, with 407 votes, and his brother was the third, with 532 votes, the highest number received. The final list of deputies from the Eure included eight others and four alternates.

Robert Lindet wrote to the Electoral Assembly during its session, on September 6: ". . . You have judged that the regeneration of France was incomplete before August 10, when you had the goodness to tell the commissioners of the Legislative Assembly that you were satisfied with my fidelity to my oath. I cannot tell you how profoundly I was moved . . . I have only one wish, namely, to terminate my labors so that I can throw myself into another work and prove my entire devotion to my fellow citizens . . . The extensive movements of our armies will stop the brigandage of the kings. The reverses we have had were due to perfidious ministers and to baseness and treason. The enemy, who wishes to march on Paris, seems to have fastened its object on Metz . . ."[25]

The Legislative Assembly met for the last time on September 20. On the same day the Convention held its first session for the purpose of organization, with only about one-half the members present. This was the auspicious day on which the Prussians were held in check at Valmy. The Convention held its first regular meeting the following day. It immediately legalized the *de facto* abolition of the monarchy of August 10 by voting unanimously for the decree abolishing the monarchy. On the next day the deputies voted that from henceforth all public documents were to

23. Arch. Nat'l. C. 178. *Procès-verbal de l'Assemblée électorale de l'Eure*; Montier, *Correspondance*, p. 261.

24. Arch. Dep't. de l'Eure, *Procès-Verbal de l'Assemblée Electorale du Département de l'Eure: 2–15 Septembre, 1792.*

25. Arch. Dep't. de l'Eure.

be dated from "Year I of the Republic." Three days later the Republic was declared to be "one and indivisible," and life and property were put under the protection of the new government. Thus was the monarchy supplanted by the national republic.

The Convention was composed of 749 members, some eighty of whom had sat in the National Assembly and about 200 in the Legislative Assembly. In the political groupings of the new assembly, about 165, mostly Girondins, sat on what was now the Right, representing the provinces, the monied, bourgeois interests of the towns and to a degree the large landowners. Their leaders were Rabaut de Saint-Etienne, Condorcet, Gaudet and Brissot. On the Left were the Montagnards, a few less in number, representing generally the democratic republicanism of the petite bourgeoisie and the workers. The Mountain was dominated by the Paris group and its leaders were Robespierre, Danton, Desmoulins, Marat, and, among the new members, Fouché, Tallien and Saint-Just. Between the two, in the Plain, or Marsh, were about 400 members whose initial leaders were Barère, Grégoire, and Siéyès. Four of the Eure deputies were grouped with the Montagnards— the two Lindets, DuRoy, and Bouillerot—Buzot was with the Girondins and the others followed his lead until he was purged on May 31-June 2, 1793, when they merged with the Plain.

An increasingly bitter struggle developed in the Convention between the Girondins and the Montagnards until the Girondins were purged in the next year on May 31 and June 2. Both groups were loyal revolutionaries and ardent patriots; both believed in the institution of private property and in the maintenance of a laissez-faire competitive economic order; neither group was a well-organized, disciplined party in the modern sense. There were policy differences between the two groups as well as sharp personality differences and rivalries between their leaders.[26]

The Girondins were the cultivated, spiritual heirs of Turgot and the Physiocrats and had read Adam Smith. These men of law and property favored an established social hierarchy, and were opposed to any governmental intervention in the economy, in-

26. M. J. Sydenham, *The Girondins* (New York: Oxford University Press, 1961), pp. 1–19, for major interpretations of the Girondins by historians. The author's interpretation of the Girondins is given in Ch. IX.

cluding the law of the maximum. After August 10 they genuinely believed that property was imperiled. They looked on the September Massacres with aversion and horror, and were strongly opposed to the domination of Paris, favoring decentralization and support of local administrative bodies. As individuals and as a group they were more theoretical and less realistic than the Montagnards; in crises they were more vacillating, timid, scrupulous, and less ruthless than their fellow revolutionaries. In the Convention they continued to frequent the salons of Mesdames Dodun, Roland, and Valaze. In sum, the Girondins now felt that the Revolution had gone far enough.

The Montagnards represented the same social and intellectual background as the Girondins. They desired the same kind of economic order, but were sensitive to the miseries of the masses and sympathetic to the lower classes; they were not opposed to temporary governmental intervention in the economy if this was necessary in the national interest and for public safety. They were dominant at the Jacobin Club in Paris, were endorsed by the Commune and were enthusiastically supported by the *sans-culottes* of the Sections.

Men of the Plain were also of the bourgeoisie. They followed an uncertain, opportunistic line; they believed in a free, unregulated economy, feared the people and abhorred violence. Their political behavior is described by Lefebvre: "As long as the Republic was in danger they thought it unwise to break with the men of August 10, especially since those men demanded measures which could be of some use until victory was won. For these reasons a few—Barère, Carnot, Lindet, Cambon—rallied to the Mountain."[27] Montier says that Lindet, the "enemy of violent solutions," in the early months of the Convention "carefully refrained from interfering in the quarrels, too frequently personal, of the leaders of the two groups, limiting himself in his committees and in his correspondence to recommending unity."[28]

The Convention had been elected to draft a constitution for a

27. Lefebvre, *The French Revolution from its Origins, op. cit.,* p. 267; see Georges Lefebvre, *La Révolution Française* (Peuples et Civilisations, Histoire Générale. Louis Halphen, Philippe Sagnac, André Aymand. troisième éd., Paris: Presses Universitaires de France, 1963), pp. 286, 430.

28. *Robert Lindet, op. cit.,* p. 39.

kingless, republican France. It also had the war to prosecute, the king to dispose of, the unfinished financial business of the Legislative Assembly, the mounting economic problems of the country, and public order and morale all to resolve.

The fate of Louis XVI was the issue overshadowing all others in the fall and early winter of 1792–3. There were three possibilities: execution, imprisonment to the end of the war, or banishment. Throughout November the Convention discussed the Report of the Committee on Legislation—of which Robert Lindet was a member—that the king was not inviolable and could be tried as a private citizen. Incriminating new evidence was discovered on November 20 in an iron chest in the Tuileries. The Montagnards were willing to condemn Louis without a trial; the Girondins resorted to delaying tactics, playing for a postponement of the trial, and then for delays in the process. Louis was formally arraigned on December 3, and the trial dragged on for a month. The Convention elected a Committee of Twenty-one on December 6, to prepare and present the *Acte énonciatif des crimes imputés à Louis XVI*. Robert Lindet was elected to this committee and was chosen its reporter. He gave the report to the Convention on December 10, in a document Mathiez describes as a "sort of historical review of the whole Revolution, in which prominence was given to the duplicity of the Crown at every critical moment."[29]

"Your Committee," reported Lindet, "thought it would be useful to preface the act of accusation with a short history of the conduct of the former king from the beginning of the Revolution. I have written it in a simple style and within the understanding of all citizens, as well as it is possible to do in the space of a day and a half." Lindet was convinced that favorable public opinion was essential to the success of the Revolution.

"Louis has been denounced before the people as a tyrant who constantly applied himself to prevent or retard the progress of liberty . . . who directed and executed a conspiracy designed to destroy the state . . . France had arrived at the point where general, widespread enlightenment and understanding of the rights of man announced a coming revolution . . . The public treasury [was] without resources, without credit, without means of preventing a

29. Mathiez, *The French Revolution, op. cit.*, p. 260.

general bankruptcy . . . Authority lacked respect for the liberty of the citizens, and power to maintain public order."

Lindet went on to trace the course of the Revolution, Louis' steady resistance, the flight to Varennes, and his behavior at critical stages. "Louis is guilty of all the crimes for which he conceived the plan from the very beginning of the Revolution, and whose demise he attempted many times. All his steps, all his procedures have been constantly directed towards the same end, namely, to recover his traditional authority, to immolate everything that resisted these efforts . . . The coalition of foreign powers, the foreign war, the sparks of the civil war, the desolation of the colonies, the internal troubles that he initiated and fomented, all these are the means he used to restore his throne, which was buried under its own debris."

Before the session adjourned at midnight, Lindet announced that the Report was not finished, for the Committee had further work to do to verify documents. Barbaroux continued the reading of the Report the next day, with the explanation: "If you do not see the same reporter at the tribune, it is because his physical powers do not permit him to continue today, after having worked three successive nights."[30]

Lindet subsequently had the substance of the Report published under the title "Outrages and Crimes of Louis, last King of the French," with the design of instructing the people. He concluded the document: "The law the most useful for the safety of the state and the most necessary for human society, is that which the Convention ought to take against Louis . . . The security and maintenance of established governments require that an assassin be punished by death. The interest of the human species and the union of men in society require that the assassin of the people and the chief of the conspiracy of kings against an entire nation be punished by death . . ."

Louis appeared before the Convention on December 11, to hear the indictment read, at which time he was invited to reply to each of the thirty-three charges of accusation.[31] He appeared for

30. *Moniteur* (Réimpression), XIV, pp. 713–718.
31. *Moniteur, op. cit.,* XIV, pp. 720 ff. The *Moniteur* reported the entire *Acte* of accusation at this time.

the second and last time on December 26 to hear Desèze, one of his three counsel, "read an eloquent defense." The Girondins attempted to save Louis' life by proposing a popular referendum, or a reprieve.

Voting in the Convention on the four critical questions began on Janaury 15, 1793, and was carried on without break for 100 hours, to the early morning of January 20. The first question was: "Is Louis guilty of conspiracy against public liberty and of plotting against the general security of the State?" All the 707 deputies present voted in the affirmative. The second question was: "Will the verdict of the National Convention against Louis Capet be referred to the people for ratification?" Of the 711 deputies voting, 424 voted no, and 287 yes, so the motion lost.[32] The third question was: "What penalty will be imposed on Louis?" Each deputy mounted the tribune and stated his vote on this question. The voting took twenty-four hours, since many of the deputies explained or elaborated their vote. Of the 721 voting, 387 voted for the death sentence, and 334 against it; twenty-six expressed themselves in favor of postponing the execution.

Among the deputies from the Eure, Buzot, after a long apologia, DuRoy, the two Lindets, and Bouillerot voted for the death sentence. Lemaréchal voted for continued imprisonment and deportation after peace was concluded with France's enemies; Vallée voted for detention until the foreign powers recognized the Republic, and execution if they invaded France; Savary voted for detention and for security measures if the Powers invaded France; Topsent was still absent because of illness. Bouillerot voted simply, "La mort." Thomas Lindet said: "I experience the painful feeling, natural to the sensitive person obliged to condemn his fellow human being, but I believe it is imprudent to encourage compassion for Louis. Does not experience prove that impunity only emboldens tyrants? I vote for death." Robert Lindet voted in these words: "I cannot recognize republicans in those who hesitate to strike down a tyrant. I vote for death."[33] On the final question:

32. *Moniteur* (Réimpression), XV, pp. 172–3. The deputies from the Eure voted as follows: Buzot, Richoux, Lemaréchal, Savary, and Dubusc voted "yes" and DuRoy, Thomas Lindet, Bouillerot, and Robert Lindet voted "no." Topsent was ill and Vallée refused to make a pronouncement.
33. *Ibid.*

"Should the execution of the judgment against Louis Capet be postponed?" the vote was 310 for and 380 against. Buzot, Richoux, Lemaréchal, Vallée, Savary and Dubusc voted for postponement, and DuRoy, the two Lindets, and Bouillerot against it.[34]

Louis went bravely to the guillotine on Sunday, January 21, 1793. Thus the regicides were born. Some fortunate enough to escape the Terror were to suffer the consequences of their votes in the Thermidorian Reaction, or, for those who lived that long, under the restoration of the Bourbons in 1815. The execution of the King drove the foreign monarchs into an implacable and irreconcilable war against revolutionary, republican France, and intensified the civil war and counter-revolution at home. But, says Lefebvre: "A king had been put to death like any ordinary man; royalty lost, never to recover, the supernatural quality that even the Revolution had not yet eradicated."[35]

The Revolution marched on. The struggle for control continued unabated between the Girondins and the Montagnards. A Committee of General Defense was formed on January 1, 1793, with twenty-one deputies, whose leading members were Brissot, Siéyès, and Barère. This forerunner to the great Committee of Public Safety was reorganized in March with twenty-four members, including Siéyès, Barère, Buzot, Cambacérès, Condorcet, Danton, Desmoulins, Gaudet, Pétion, Robespierre, and Vergniaud.

The Girondins early in the Convention committed themselves to a war of propaganda and of territorial expansion. Military victories and effective propaganda resulted in the annexation of Savoy, Nice, the Rhineland and part of the Lowlands by midwinter. The propaganda decree of November 19, 1792, promised fraternity and military aid to all peoples wishing to "recover their liberty." The war went well for France for a time after Valmy. By November 28 the Austrians had evacuated Belgium and the Convention at once opened the Scheldt and Antwerp to international

34. *Ibid.*, p. 254. The recording of this vote was illuminating, as given in the *Moniteur*: Members 749, Dead 1, Remainder 748, Absent on Mission 17, Absent because of illness 21, Did not wish to vote 12, Remaining voters 690, one-half of voters 345, Absolute majority 346, For the postponement 310, Against the postponement, 380.

35. Lefebvre, *The French Revolution, op. cit.*, p. 272.

commerce. Here was a direct challenge to the commercial and naval interests of England.

The second propaganda decree of December 15 went much further and into greater detail than the former one. The advancing republican generals were to carry the Revolution with them, liberate the peoples, abolish feudalism, establish provisional governments under French patronage, prepare the sovereign people for self-government, and supervise the establishment of their own free and popular governments. The earlier decree of 1790 renouncing wars of conquest and interference in the domestic affairs of neighbor states was hereby repudiated. The Montagnards by now were not averse to a war of propaganda and annexation although they continued to criticize the incompetent conduct of the war in the hands of the Girondin politicians and generals.

Chauvelin, the French ambassador in England, on the day of Louis' execution had been given eight days in which to leave the country and on February 1 France declared war on England and Holland. It declared war on Spain on March 7. By the end of 1793 England had formed the First Coalition by concluding treaties with Austria, Prussia, Sardinia and Holland. Robert Lindet had opposed the declaration of war on England on practical grounds. When the proposal was made by Brissot, a reporter of the Committee on ᴅiplomacy, Lindet said "The *rapporteur* is not informed as to the condition of our navy: we have no means of attacking our new enemies. We do not even have the means to support a defensive war."[36]

The Convention decreed a Levy of 300,000 men on February 24. This forerunner of the famous *levée en masse* put all males from eighteen to forty, unmarried or widowers without children, under permanent requisition until the 300,000 were actually recruited, provided for the amalgamation of the regular and volunteer troops, fixed the contingent to be raised by each department, and stipulated the means of providing clothing, equipment and provisions for the troops. For purposes of the Levy, the population of the Eure was given as 406,000, of Paris as 950,000 and all of France, as 27,182,000.[37]

36. Montier, *Robert Lindet, op. cit.*, p. 53.
37. Arch. Nat., AF 11, carton 9, folder 55.

The Convention decreed an Extraordinary Revolutionary Tribunal on March 10, 1793. Apparently this had been proposed by Danton and was presented to the Convention by Robert Lindet for the Committee on Legislation. There were to be five judges, a jury, and a public prosecutor with two assistants, all to be appointed by the Convention. The Tribunal was to have wide powers to prosecute and condemn all enemies of the state. The judges were to direct the inquiry and apply the law after the jurors had declared upon the facts "publicly, aloud, and by absolute majority of votes." A commission of six members of the Convention was to examine all documents and draft and present indictments to the Tribunal, maintain a regular correspondence with the public prosecutor and the judges concerning all public suits dispatched to the court, and render an accounting thereof to the Convention. The property of persons condemned to death was to be confiscated by the state, with provision made for their widows and children if these had no property. The judgments of the Tribunal were to be executed without the right of appeal to the Court of Cassation.[38]

Robert Lindet, prior to the vote on the proposed decree, presented something of a substitute, summarized as follows in *Le Moniteur*: "The extraordinary tribunal will be composed of nine members, named by the Convention. They will be subject to no kind of direction. They will achieve conviction by all means possible. The tribunal may divide itself into two sections. There shall always be one member on duty in the meeting place, to receive denunciations. The tribunal will judge those who have been sent to it by order of the Convention. It can prosecute directly those who, by *incivisme*, would abandon or neglect the exercise of their functions; those who, by their behavior or by the manifestation of their opinions attempt to mislead the people; those whose conduct or writing, or positions they held under the ancien régime, recall the usurped prerogatives of the despots."[39]

Vergniaud vigorously opposed this proposal: "When a proposal

38. *Moniteur* XV, 676. See Stewart, *A Documentary Survey, op. cit.,* pp. 409–412.
39. *Moniteur*, XV, p. 681: "A great many members of the Left applauded this proposal and demanded that it be considered. A lively demonstration manifested itself in the opposing party."

is made to us for the establishment of an inquisition more formidable than that of Venice we would all rather die than consent to it. I demand that the discussion begin on the [earlier] proposals presented." "Plusieurs voix: Fermez la discussion, et mettez aux voix." Cambon and Barère then spoke against Lindet's proposal as an attack upon the free press and freedom of opinion in general. The Convention voted unanimously to have the jurors chosen by the Convention but from the various departments. The report concluded: "The Convention then adopted successively, and after little discussion, the other articles in the proposal of Lindet," that is, the Committee report.[40]

Robert Lindet felt moved to defend himself against the critical attacks upon the harsh and extreme proposal that he had made on his own responsibility in the Convention. This took the popular form of a pamphlet, "Robert Lindet à ses concitoyens," published in Paris on March 30, 1793. "One should judge severely a leader who has endangered or compromised the security of the army by treason, by negligence or by *incivisme* . . . I have confused nothing: he who deserts or neglects his functions, to aid the conspirators and the counter-revolutionaries, ought to be tried and punished . . . I have not attacked the freedom of the press: this freedom applies only to republicans. I am forced to consider manifestation of opinions in favor of royalism as a crime . . . Royalists and fanatics should have no form of freedom: they should find neither safety nor asylum in France.

"The freedom of the press should be unlimited, but we should not guarantee it to our enemies . . . Furthermore, I believe that a tribunal which investigates and tries a case before the nation, under the eyes of the people, under the supervision of the representatives of the people, ought not be shackled. It judges under the eyes and in the presence of its own judges. This tribunal will be judged itself by public opinion every time it renders a judgment. I have presumed to find in the nature of its functions, in the greatest possible publicity and in the highest sense of responsibility, a sure guarantee of the wise, firm, just and severe behavior of these trustees of public confidence."[41]

40. *Ibid.*, pp. 681, 684.
41. Montier, *Robert Lindet, op. cit.*, pp. 57–58.

This dangerous and specious argument, even though prompted by the distress of revolutionary France under the attacks of the royalist coalition, was recalled by Lindet's political enemies in the Thermidorian Reaction when those associated with the Terror were under attack. In his *Mémoires*, La Révellière-Lepeaux (1753–1824), one of his most persistent attackers, in recalling Lindet's presentation of the proposal of the Committee on Legislation for the Revolutionary Tribunal, described the "bitter, cold and cruel smile of R. Lindet, *rapporteur*." Lindet's biographer comments: "The truth is that Lindet had a sort of permanent grin [tick] on his face which gave him a sarcastic expression."[42]

The French Army of the North under Dumouriez was suffering reverses in these early March days. Dumouriez' loyalty was suspect and it is likely that he was intriguing with the Orleanists for the establishment of an Orleanist dynasty, with Louis-Philippe as king and himself as major-domo. After Dumouriez' defeat at Maestricht he retreated into Belgium, where the Belgians were in revolt against the French. The Army of the North was badly defeated at Neerwinden on March 18–19, and by March 31 the French had completely evacuated Belgium. Tensions mounted in the Convention and restlessness grew in Paris.

The Convention decreed on March 8, on Danton's motion, to send two Commissioners from the Convention to each of the forty-eight Sections in Paris to inform them of the military situation in Belgium and recruit all citizens capable of bearing arms. Robert Lindet and Jean-Baptiste Mailhe (1754–1834) from the Haute-Garonne, were sent to the Section de Panthéon.[43] Carnot, on the same day, for the Committee of General Defense and War, proposed sending eighty-two Commissioners from the Convention, in pairs, into the forty-one regions proposed for the exercise of their mission. These Commissioners were to inform the people of the dangers threatening the nation, and were given wide powers, under the decree of February 24, to levy troops and take other measures essential to the national defense. The proposal was adopted.

42. *Ibid.*, p. 59.
43. F.-A. Aulard, *Recueil des Actes du Comité du Salut Public Avec La Correspondance officielle Des Représentants en Mission* (Paris: Imprimerie Nationale, 1889), II, p. 286.

On April 6, 1793, the Convention decreed the formation of a Committee of Public Safety, as an emergency executive committee to supplant the large, unwieldly and ineffective Committee of General Defense, whose deliberations had been public. The new Committee of nine members was granted wide powers: it was to supervise the Executive Council of six ministers, was to deliberate in secret, had an extraordinary special fund of 100,000 livres at its disposal for which it need not account, and, under urgent circumstances, was to assume responsibility for both internal and external affairs. It was to report weekly in writing to the Convention on its activities and on the state of the nation. The original committee was established for a one-month term. Responsible to the Convention as its emergency executive arm, it came to dominate the Convention during the great crisis of the Revolution in the Government of the Terror.

Barère was the first deputy elected to the Committee with 360 votes. Danton and six others of the Dantonist wing of the Mountain were elected, and the Committee was known as the Danton committee. Renewed each month, this Committee served until July 10, when Danton and others were replaced. Other than Barère and Danton (233 votes), those elected in April were Delmas (347), Bréard (325), Cambon (278), Jean deBry (227), Guyton-Morveau (202), Treilhard (160), and Delacroix of Eure-et-Loir (151). Jean de Bry declined to serve because of health, and Robert Lindet, who had received 122 votes on the original ballot, was elected to replace him. All of the nine, excepting Lindet, had been members of the Committee of General Defense. Barère and Lindet were the two not closely associated with the Dantonists in the Convention.

Lawyers predominated in this first Committee. Bréard was a magistrate, Barère, Danton, Delacroix, Lindet and Treilhard were lawyers, and Guyton-Morveau was both a lawyer and a chemist. Delmas was a military officer in the National Guard. The Committee met and organized itself on April 7, with Guyton-Morveau president, Bréard vice-president, and Barère and Lindet secretaries. In the special responsibilities and division of labor adopted on April 10, Cambon, Guyton-Morveau and Lindet were given correspondence, the interior, subsistance, finance, distribution of work in the Committee, and the supervision of the bureaux, Delmas and Delacroix the department of war, Barère and Danton foreign affairs, and Treilhard and Bréard the navy.[44] The Committee plunged immediately into its work. It held 116 meetings between April 7 and the proscription of the Girondins on June 2.

The Convention on April 9 decreed the establishment of "Representatives on Mission," three to each army, with very great powers, both in the armies and in their regions.[45] A decree of April 8 had laid down the regulations concerning the correspondence between the Committee of Public Safety and the deputies already on mission. Lindet, on behalf of the Committee, on April 21 wrote to the Representatives to the Army of the Moselle and Rhine, detailing their responsibilities: ". . . We beg you to give all your attention to execute the law and prevent every kind of disorder and convulsion; it is necessary to establish the national credit, and it is by confidence that this will be done. You realize how much we count on your experience, your enlightenment and your activity . . . The decree of April 8 is a great measure of politics and of confidence, but we should not conceal from you that it was commanded by necessity . . ."[46] Lindet wrote for the Committee to the Representatives on Mission in the Gard and l'Herault on April 23: "Citizens our Colleagues, we learn that a serious fermentation reigns in the Departments of Gard and the Bouches-du-Rhône. We beg you to concert your efforts at once with our colleague deputies at Marseilles. End these extreme agitations, which can be fatal to public tranquillity, by all the means which are at your disposition and under the powers delegated to you. Preserve the southern departments from the calamities which afflict the departments of the west. Be the pacifiers of our citizens . . . Reunite them and direct their efforts against the enemies of liberty."[47]

Marat was the object of a Girondin attack by Gaudet in the Convention on April 12. Gaudet, after a lengthy reply to Robespierre's denunciation of the Girondins for alleged complicity with Dumouriez and the Duke of Orleans, proposed that Marat be

44. Aulard, *Recueil*, III, 132, 182.
45. Stewart, *A Documentary Survey, op. cit.*, pp. 425–6.
46. Aulard, *Recueil*, III, 372–3.
47. *Ibid.*, 410–411.

cited before the Revolutionary Tribunal. The charge was that
Marat, as president of the Paris Jacobin Club, had signed a circular of April 5 to the club's affiliates in France accusing the
Girondins as counter-revolutionaries. After a violent debate the
motion was passed in an oral vote.[48]

Thomas Lindet was absent at the time of the vote. Robert Lindet
voted against the *mis en accusation* in a lengthy statement in
which he said: "No, Marat has served his country, he has served
the human race; he is the outspoken friend of the people and the
enemy of tyrants; he has scorned and rejected wealth; he has
braved perils; he has risked his liberty and his life to combat
despotism and proclaim the rights of man . . . For myself, I would
consider myself guilty of a crime against public liberty and the
national representation if I voted a decree of accusation against a
representative of the people who has served his country, fought
despotism and unmasked traitors. You have refused to listen to
your colleague [Marat]; you are not even sure that he is the author
of the copies that have been read, and which the public may
accuse you of misunderstanding the intention."[49]

Marat was acquitted by the friendly Revolutionary Tribunal in
eulogistic terms and under the influence of a popular demonstration. The acquittal was reported to the Convention and Marat
returned to his seat, more popular than ever.[50] The immunity of
the deputies had been breached and the Girondins were soon to
rue the day.

The Convention decreed the first Law of the Maximum on
May 4, establishing a uniform price for grain and a legal price
for bread, though the table of prices varied according to local
circumstances. The law proved to be ineffective, partly because of
the unwillingness or the failure of local officials to administer and
enforce it.

The political struggle for power in the Convention between the

48. *Moniteur*, XVI, 127–136; 136–151. The *Moniteur* gave the vote as
220 for the motion, 92 against, 7 for adjournment, more than 48 abstentions, and about 300 deputies on mission. cf. Mathiez, *The French Revolution, op. cit.*, p. 315. Mathiez gives the vote as 226 for, 93 against, and 47
abstentions.
49. Montier, *Robert Lindet, op. cit.*, pp. 71–72.
50. *Moniteur*, XVI, 216; 220–1.

Girondins and the Montagnards was coming to its climax in April and May. The Commune of Paris was extremely partisan in its support of the Montagnards. In May rumours spread that the Commune was threatening to dissolve the Convention in order to get rid of the Girondins. The latter responded by denouncing the Commune, by trying to arouse the departments against the capital, by planning to dissolve the Commune, and by proposing to move the capital from Paris. In mid-May the Girondins put through a decree establishing a Commission of Twelve, filled by Girondins, to investigate and to quell popular disorders in Paris. This Commission arrested Hébert and Varlet, popular with the masses. The Commune replied by petitioning the Convention on May 25 to expel the Girondins. The Commission itself was suppressed by the Convention on May 27, but on the following day the Girondins, by desperate measures, succeeded in having it restored.

This prompted the Sections to prepare an insurrection. A Central Insurrectionary Committee of nine men took over control both of the Commune and the National Guard, naming Hanriot as its commander-in-chief. The Insurrectionary Committee declared itself *en permanence* on May 30. When the Convention assembled on May 31 it found itself surrounded by 30,000 Parisians. The Convention proceeded to abolish the Commission of Twelve and the mob dispersed. On June 1 a new petition against thirty-two Girondins was introduced in the Convention and on June 2 a mob of 80,000 under Hanriot, supported by sixty cannon, surrounded the Convention, to force it to act on the petition.[51] The Convention finally decreed the arrest of twenty-nine deputies, including the two ministers Lebrun and Clavière and the twelve members of the Commission, among whom were Vergniaud, Brissot, Gaudet, Gensonné, Isnard, and Barbaroux. The arrested Girondins were put under surveillance in their own homes. The Montagnards had triumphed as masters of the Convention, subject to the pressures of the Commune and the domination of the Committee of Public Safety. The revolts in the departments were gathering momentum even before the purge of the Girondins. Lyons had thrown off Jacobin rule on May 29; Marseilles followed after

51. George Rudé, *op. cit.*, pp. 120 ff. for the role of the Commune and the Sections in the purging of the Girondins.

June 2 and by mid-June over sixty departments were in rebellion.

Robert Lindet, apparently alarmed by the factions and the alleged intrigues of the Girondins, had voted with the majority on June 2 for the arrest of their leaders. Shortly after the adoption of the hastily-prepared Constitution on June 24, he issued a forty-seven page defense of his vote. "A conspiracy against the republic has existed for a long time in the bosom of the Convention; a plan was undertaken as vast as that which Louis conceived when he wished to enslave France. Fanaticism was excited in the departments, the administrative corps was corrupted, the generals were won over; Paris was to be destroyed." He went on to justify the revolution of August 10, giving a detailed résumé of subsequent events in 1792 and 1793, implicating the Girondins as conspirators. Lindet named names and he accused those identified of trying to rehabilitate their reputations in the departments after their defeats in the Convention. He spoke of the Roland home as the center of intrigue, named the Girondin-dominated Committee of General Defense as responsible for adding Spain to the enemies of France, and explained the establishment of the Revolutionary Tribunal: "The numbers of conspirators had become so frightening that the National Convention was obliged to decree the establishment of a revolutionary tribunal to try those guilty of crimes of conspiracy and counter-revolution. The interest of the republic demanded the most prompt organization of this tribunal."[52]

Lindet accused the Girondins of procrastination in the preparation of the Constitution, particularly singling out Vergniaud, Barbaroux, Pétion, and Condorcet, as members of the Committee on the Constitution. The Girondin Committee of General Defense had sanctioned the federal system: "Gensonné claimed that each deputy should consider himself ambassador of his department, and the will of each deputation could not be influenced, changed, or modified by the will of the other deputations."[53] Lindet recapitu-

---

52. Robert Lindet, *Exposition des Motifs qui ont déterminé Robert Lindet, député du département de l'Eure à la Convention nationale, à voter pour l'arrestation de 32 membres de la convention nationale* (Paris: R. Vatar, 1793), pp. 3–4; 36.

53. This quotation is from a shorter exposition on the same theme: Robert Lindet. *Exposition des motifs*, etc., (Paris: De l'Imprimerie du *Journal des Débats*, 1793), p. 16.

lated the events in Paris and in the Convention in May, leading up to June 2. He called Isnard the "base slave of his faction . . . The insurrection of the department of Paris prevented the accomplishment of the schemes of the conspirators, as the revolution of August 10 had saved France from the yoke of the allied despots." He then called the recently-adopted Constitution a "masterpiece of reason and humanity." He reported that after June 2: "Buzot, Lesage, Louvet, Gorsas and several others of their accomplices had gone to Caen. General Wimpfen of the Army of the Côtes de la Manche had gone over to them. They proclaimed civil war in the Departments of Calvados and the Eure. They negotiated with the administrators of many departments for the purpose of igniting the fire of civil war."[54]

The Constitution had been hastily completed and adopted on June 24, largely for the purpose of disarming and pacifying the federalists, as well as for reassuring the propertied classes that property rights were secure. This Constitution did not differ greatly from the one submitted by Condorcet on February 15. It was democratic in that it called for universal male suffrage. It included the Declaration of Rights proposed by Robespierre on April 24, although it omitted four articles by whose provisions poor citizens would receive tax exemptions and economic support from the fortunes of the rich. This Jacobin Constitution was overwhelmingly ratified in the summer by the citizens who voted. The vote was 1,801,918 for and 11,610 against, but 100,000 of the affirmative voters voted for it only on condition of liberating the arrested Girondin deputies, recall of the Representatives on Mission, and the suppression of the Maximum.[55] It was not intended that the Constitution would go into effect during the national crisis.

The Committee of Public Safety was reorganized on July 10. The discredited, conciliatory Danton was not re-elected. The nine elected were Barère, Jeanbon Saint-André, Gasparin, Couthon, Hérault de Sechelles, Thuriot, Prieur de la Marne, Saint-Just, and Lindet. In the voting Barère and Jeanbon Saint-André received the highest number of votes with 192 each; Lindet was last on the list with 100 votes. Gasparin resigned on July 27 because of ill

54. These quotations are from the longer version, pp. 40, 43, 44, 45.
55. Mathiez, *Girondins et Montagnards, op. cit.*, p. 103.

health and was replaced by Robespierre. Of the new members Gasparin was a lawyer, Couthon an army captain, Hérault de Sechelles a magistrate of noble family, Thuriot a lawyer and magistrate, Prieur de la Marne and Robespierre lawyers; Saint-Just had a degree in law but was really without profession.

The summer months continued to be turbulent. On July 8 the Convention, on recommendation of the Committee of Public Safety, had outlawed the leaders of the rebellion in the departments. The federalist movement had pretty much collapsed after June 24 with the adoption of the Constitution and the popular referendum. The rebellion developed, however, into a royalist movement in Marseilles, Lyons, Toulon and Bordeaux. In the Vendée it took the violent form of a royalist civil war and counter-revolution, under the leadership of the nobles, and the non-juring priests. During the summer, Metz, Valenciennes and Condé fell to the Austrians and Prussians. The Vendéans were generally successful and the English Admiral Hood was welcomed into the harbor of Toulon on August 28.

Robert Lindet got his first assignment outside Paris when the Convention named him on June 7 to join Albitte and Dubois-Crancé, regular Representatives-on-Mission to the Army of the Alps, commanded by Kellermann, for the purpose of restoring order in the rebellious city of Lyons.[56] He had requested the assignment. As early as March 15 the earlier Representatives, Basire, Rovère and Legendre, had reported the federalist activities in Lyons to the Convention, mentioning the role of the nobles, the counter-revolutionary propaganda in the *Journal de la Ville de Lyon*, and the interfering intrigues of the royal court of Turin.[57] Donald Greer, in his *The Incidence of the Terror During the French Revolution* traces the beginnings of counter-revolution in Lyons back to 1790 when some citizens of that city were working with royalist conspirators in the *Midi*. He gives details of plotting in 1789–1792 and reports that Lyons became the "refuge for the nobles of the Cévennes, and, in fact, for malcontents from all parts of Southern France. The banker Couderc credited the rumor that there were 20,000 strangers in the city in April, 1792; Dubois-

56. Aulard, *Recueil des Actes*, IV, 432.
57. *Ibid.*, II, 384–7.

Crancé wrote in May that the place was infested with refactory priests . . ."[58] Greer attributes the revolt in Lyons to an internal class struggle in this great industrial city between the reactionaries and the proletariat, the earliest victims of the industrial revolution in France. Godechot says the city had become overpopulated by the eve of the Revolution.[59]

Unemployed and starving silk workers became strong supporters of the Jacobins and their radical leader, Chalier. Although there was a Girondin mayor in the winter of 1792–3, the municipal council was controlled by the Jacobins. Bertrand, a Jacobin, was inaugurated mayor on March 9. "Once in power," writes Greer, "the Jacobins began domiciliary visits, wholesale arrests and the formation of a revolutionary army to be paid for by a tax of five million francs on the rich. Little else was needed to produce the anti-Jacobin insurrection of May 29."[60]

The administration of the Department of Rhône-et-Loire supported the Girondins in this uprising. The Girondins and the royalist Sections, with bloody violence, captured the Hôtel de Ville and replaced the legal Jacobin government, imprisoning its leaders —Chalier was subsequently executed on July 16. This successful Girondin insurrection of May 29 was not known in Paris until June 2.[61] Albitte and Dubois-Crancé sent an urgent report on the crisis in Lyons to the Committee of Public Safety on June 5 from Grenoble. They stated that Lyons was sending thirty-two commissioners to the Convention to win approval of its program, which included the intention to "destroy the patriotic clubs as anarchists." The Representatives on Mission said the commissioners were planning to denounce the agreement made by the administrative corps in the presence of the Representatives on Mission, and that the commissioners planned to incriminate the Representatives. The latter named Megins, the *procureur general*, as the mainspring of the rebellious disorders. "The result of this movement is that true

58. Donald Greer, *The Incidence of the Terror During the French Revolution* (Cambridge: Harvard University Press, 1935), pp. 58–59.

59. Godechot, *La Contre-Révolution, op. cit.*, p. 253.

60. Greer, *op. cit.*, p. 60.

61. Aulard, *Histoire Politique, op. cit.*, pp. 436–7; For the insurrection in Lyons also see Godechot, *La Contre-Révolution, op. cit.*, pp. 253–8.

patriotism is crushed and the aristocracy will triumph." They also reported that the army warehouses had been destroyed.[62]

The Convention on June 7, the same day it deputized Lindet to join them, decreed full powers to the Representatives on Mission to the Army of the Alps to restore calm and public tranquillity in Lyons, subject to a *compte rendu* to the Convention.[63] The Committee of Public Safety on the same day instructed Albitte and Dubois-Crancé to use the order to send a contingent of the Army of the Alps to Lyons with the "greatest prudence."[64]

Lindet had a hostile reception by the municipal authorities on his arrival in Lyons. They refused to recognize his mandate and threatened to arrest him. His first report to the Committee of Public Safety on June 9 expressed vividly his difficulties.[65] "Arrived at Lyons at six o'clock in the morning; I presented my passport to the commandant who showed me an order to present me immediately." Lindet, however, had difficulty in making contact with the authorities and in obtaining a safe conduct. "I was reproached for having proposed the decree to establish the revolutionary tribunal, and to have voted in the affair of June 1 . . . The session [of the General Council of the commune which had usurped power on May 29] met at five o'clock and adjourned at ten o'clock. They complained bitterly of what our colleagues [the Representatives on Mission] have done and said in Lyons. They repeated phrases that had made an impression. They deliberated whether they could recognize me as a representative of the people —that the Convention was no more guilty than all its members. The president of the Commune demanded that I be denied recognition. Several demanded that I be put under arrest and detained at Lyons until they knew what was to happen to the thirty-two deputies put under arrest by the Convention. This proposal was defeated . . .

"They informed me that there was uneasiness concerning my principles and my way of thinking. This gave me little anxiety.

62. Aulard, *Recueil*, IV, 459–460.
63. Arch. Nat'l., A. F. 11, 43, dossier 340.
64. Aulard, *Recueil*, IV, 476.
65. Arch. Nat., 11, 43, dossier 340, pièce 24, Affaires de Lyon. Correspondance de Robert Lindet envoyé à Lyon après la journée de 31 Mai 1793; Aulard, *Recueil*, IV, 496–7.

They adjourned in order to consult tomorrow with all the Sections . . . whether or not to verify my powers.

"To foment trouble and maintain division and distrust, it is publicized here that there exists a party which would institute a monarchy in half of France and abandon the other half. An extraordinary agent [sent to Paris], returned to Lyons, has announced the existence of such a party. This chimera creates fear . . . Such scurrilous imposters do a great deal of harm. The Committee of Public Safety has not an instant to lose in giving its attention to a pressing task. It must give an exposition of the causes for the decree of arrest [of the Girondins] . . . It must enlighten France."

This calm and sober letter from the conciliatory Lindet, in the face of hostility and danger, was followed by a second letter on the next day[66] in which he commented on the violent insurrection of the Girondins and royalists on May 29 resulting in the overthrow of the Jacobin Commune. "The sections deliberated yesterday . . . The General Council [of the Commune] informed me at six o'clock that it had prepared an address to the National Convention that demands the report on the decree [of June 2] and that this address will be printed and sent to the departments and to the principal cities . . .

"I have heard the most serious complaints against the Representatives of the people. But no one has wanted to give me any details of May 29. I shall know today whether I am to be recognized or not. If not, I shall return to my post . . . Order and silence reign here. I presume that my trip here will be useless. Perhaps what I have said will make some impression . . . I can not give a detailed report of my observations until I am in Paris.

"If this state of affairs continues for long, we will be the prey of foreigners. In order to support the armies and to be successful, courage and enthusiasm are necessary, and this enthusiasm is only inspired by the emotions of unity and of confidence. The calm in the interior can only be a happy omen when it is the product of harmony and of the general security. The calm which Lyons enjoys is rather the stillness of passions (*le silence des passions*)

66. Arch. Nat., A. F. 11, 43, dossier 340, pièce 25.

than the effect of common satisfaction. The force of arms has decided everything . . .

"Hasten, Representatives, to enlighten France, to put before it a faithful picture of what has happened. Declare the good and the bad with the same impartiality. Inform France of what led to and prepared the events of June 2."

Lindet presented himself to the Departmental Assembly on the morning of June 10, to seek a hearing. The sizeable assembly put off this request for other business but finally agreed to receive Lindet at five o'clock. At that time he requested the registration of the decree that had ordered him to go to Lyons. After a long discussion the session was adjourned until the next day so that the provisional General Council and the will of the Sections might be consulted. In his letter to the Committee of Public Safety on June 11, reporting these efforts, Lindet wrote: "It is prudent to accelerate the exposition of the causes of the decree of arrest. But it is also urgent to fix upon a Constitution."[67]

Lindet reported to the Committee of Public Safety on June 12 that the Departmental Assembly had accused him of being responsible for the revolutionary tribunal at Lyons. An article in a paper in Lyons had published a letter from Dubois-Crancé to the Committee of Public Safety, relating the happenings in Lyons and announcing the march of troops on Lyons. Lindet commented: "This measure seems to me to be unfortunate and precipitate. I believe that all violence is wrong when no efforts have been made to reunite minds and achieve reconciliation. I believe it is a sacred duty to use all means of conciliation before employing the force of arms . . . I had hoped to return to Paris. Now I believe my duty is to stay in Lyons. You recognize . . . that my sole desire to be useful prompts me to postpone my earlier decision." He said he had dispatched an urgent message by a gendarme to Albitte and Dubois-Crancé. "I await impatiently the reply from Dubois-Crancé and Albitte." He then gave the formula that he considered wise and useful in resolving situations such as that in Lyons. "Negotiate, gain time, conciliate the minds, trust in the return of confidence which cannot be misled for long, exorcise the storm, settle everything by the use of good

67. Arch. Nat., A. F. 11, 43, dossier 340, pièce 26.

judgment." Unfortunately, the rebellion had gone too far and passions were too inflamed for such a reasonable approach.[68]

Lindet wrote every day to the Committee of Public Safety, continuing to insist that the Convention complete the Constitution, explain the reasons for the June 2 arrest of the Girondin deputies, and make a full public *exposé* of the state of affairs in France. He wrote on June 14 "the object of my mission is fulfilled as far as it is possible to be." He had persuaded the Representatives on Mission to the Army of the Alps to refrain from marching the army on Lyons. The Convention on July 17, on the recommendation of the Committee of Public Safety, decreed that the *procureur-général-syndic* of the Department of Rhône-et-Loire, the *procureur-syndic* of the district of Lyons, and the *procureur* of the Commune of Lyons were temporarily suspended and were to appear before the Convention. The decree also instructed Lindet to return to the Convention so that it might have accurate information on the situation in Lyons.

Lindet was never officially received by the insurrectionary authorities in Lyons. He was in Paris by June 21, for on that day he gave his report to the Convention.[69] He expressed the hope: "If the new authorities in Lyons hold the reins of administration with firmness there will be nothing to fear for liberty." Des Essarts speaks of these as words "full of mildness."[70] Lindet had already told his colleagues on the Committee of Public Safety that it was necessary to "satisfy wounded feelings, calm the minds, temporize, and above all avoid all violent measures."[71]

Lindet wrote a long report of his mission to Lyons to the citizens of Bernay on June 20 in which he said: "France can be destroyed by Frenchmen. You love your country, you know that there must be a rallying point. If one breaks with the Convention what will become of the government? What will happen to our armies? We know that public services cannot be interrupted for a single day . . . The [local] administrations have

68. *Ibid.*, pièce 27.
69. *Moniteur*, XVI, pp. 671, 706–7.
70. Emmanuel Des Essarts, "Robert Lindet," *La Révolution Française*, 1882, 675.
71. Montier, *Robert Lindet, op. cit.*, p. 94.

not been elected to foment disorders and incite civil war."[72]

The Convention finally laid siege to rebellious and recalcitrant Lyons on August 18 and eventually took the stubbornly-defended city on October 9. The Convention decreed on October 12: "The city of Lyons will be destroyed. Every dwelling of the rich will be demolished. Only the homes of the poor, of slaughtered or proscribed patriots, factory buildings, and monuments dedicated to humanity and to public instruction will remain. The name of Lyons will be expunged from the list of cities of the Republic. What remains will henceforth be known as the Freed City (*Ville-Affranchie*)."[73]

Lindet was deputized by the Committee of Public Safety to propose a decree in the Convention on June 26 aimed at rebellious magistrates, administrators and citizens in the insurrectionary areas, designed to have them retract their disloyalty and return to their republican obligations. In his introduction to this decree he said: "Citizens, a huge conspiracy has been plotted against liberty; you have halted it in smiting the conspirators, many of whom spread themselves through the departments for the purpose of igniting the civil war. The [local] administrators have supported them; they have sounded the tocsin of counter-revolution; they would rend the republic. This is not an insurrection, it is a rebellion. You cannot, however, strike all the guilty for they are too numerous; begin by enlightening them. I am charged to propose a message addressed to the French . . . to reestablish order and public tranquillity . . . wishing to summons all Frenchmen to reunite under the Constitution which is presented for their acceptance . . ."[74] By the decree all administrators, magistrates, judges, and all other public functionaries who had misled the people, were to retract within three days after the publication of the decree. Those refusing and continuing to foment civil disobedience and insurrection were to be declared traitors and were to be punished as such. Rebellious departmental officers of the Eure were among those at whom this decree was aimed. Robert

72. *Ibid.*, pp. 102–3.
73. Aulard, *Histoire Politique, op. cit.*, 445.
74. *Moniteur*, XVI, 757.

Lindet was able to report to the Convention on June 27 that these particular officers had retracted.[75]

Lindet received another important assignment soon after his return from Lyons. The bloody, troublesome and stubborn Vendéan civil war had begun in March and was to be a thorn in the side of the Convention for more than two years. This was both an insurrection of devout peasants and non-juring priests and a counter-revolution of nobles, using the peasants in the desperate effort to restore the throne.[76]

A much shorter, less well-organized insurrection was under way in Calvados and the Eure. The Committee of Public Safety began to discuss the rebellious situation in the Eure on May 30. Buzot, from the Eure and one of the Girondin deputies arrested on June 2, had escaped from house custody and was fomenting the federalist uprising in these two departments. Generally given the cold shoulder in Evreux, he had gone to Caen on June 12, where an insurrectionary government, the Central Assembly of the Resistance to Oppression, overthrew the legitimate government and took over control on June 30. The two Representatives on Mission with the Army of the Côtes de Cherbourg, Romme and Prieur (de la Côte-D'Or) were arrested and jailed in Caen.[77]

Vergniaud, one of the proscribed Girondin deputies, issued a lengthy printed proclamation, dated Paris, June 28, but printed at Nîmes, and addressed to Barère and Lindet. It accused them bitterly for being responsible for the revolts in the departments. "I denounce you to France as imposters and assassins . . . My death [he was brought before the Revolutionary Tribunal on October 30, 1793, condemned to death, and executed on the following day] will be the last crime of our modern *décemvirs*. Far from fearing this I long for it. Soon the people, enlightened by this, will be delivered from their horrible tyranny."[78]

---

75. Montier, *Robert Lindet, op. cit.*, pp. 106–109.
76. Godechot, *La Contre-Révolution, op. cit.*, Ch. XI.
77. Arch. Dept. Eure, 12 L 22, 23. Placards, Posters, Proclamations *re* Federalism in Calvados and the Eure. See Sydenham, *op. cit.*, p. 196, "True federalism apparently appealed to no one in Roland's circle except Buzot . . ."
78. Arch. Nat., 11, 46 dossier 358.

Lindet, well-informed of the disaffection in the Eure, had at first opposed sending troops to quell the uprising, but circumstances convinced him that force might be necessary. He proposed to the Committee of Public Safety that a small contingent of three or four thousand troops be sent to General Wimpfen, commander-in-chief of the Army of the Côtes de Cherbourg, to be used to put down the insurrection, but with the reservation that the Representatives on Mission with that army make every effort to negotiate before resorting to force. The Committee, after Lindet had needled it in the Convention on July 4 by stating: "The inaction of the Committee of Public Safety and the Executive Council is reprehensible . . . Citizens, when will you stop the progress of the rebellion? . . ."[79] recommended Lindet's proposal to the Convention on the same day, and this was approved. The Committee of Public Safety then inquired who might be sent to execute the decree. Lindet replied: "I, myself, if you wish." This offer was "joyfully accepted." DuRoy, also of the Eure, asked to be associated with Lindet and this wish also was granted. The Convention authorized the minister of war to provide troops and munitions for the enterprise. The troops were to follow Lindet and DuRoy, who were sent "to bring the citizens back to obedience and respect for the laws by the means of persuasion and instruction."[80] Twenty-thousand livres were put at their disposal. In the meantime, General Wimpfen had defected on July 2, had accepted the command of the insurrectionary forces, and threatened to march on Paris.

The Convention, in conformity with the recommendation of the Committee of Public Safety, ordered the two special commissioners to go to the Eure on July 9 and to "take all measures of general security necessary under the circumstances."[81] Lindet went to Mantes on July 11 to accelerate the preparation of the Parisian troops who were "full of ardour and eager to measure swords with the federalist army."[82] In the evening he visited the

79. *Moniteur*, XVII, 47–48.
80. Montier, *Robert Lindet, op. cit.*, pp. 115–116.
81. Aulard, *Recueil*, V, 218.
82. Montier, *Robert Lindet, op. cit.*, p. 118.

popular society where "we had proofs of the patriotism of the good *sans-culottes* of Mantes, mostly laborers and artisans."[83] DuRoy arrived at Vernon on the same day and found that the ammunition was ready.

Puisy, aide-de-camp of Wimpfen, had arrived in Evreux to take command of 3,000 insurrectionary troops of the department. He marched on Vernon, where DuRoy and the Convention's troops were assembled, stopping en route at the chateau of Brecourt where his men got drunk on cider. DuRoy launched a surprise attack at Pacy-sur-Eure on July 13, and the insurgents were routed. No blood was spilt and no lives lost. This engagement became known in the countryside as the "battle without tears."[84] The Girondin followers were effectively crushed. Puisy left Evreux on July 14, taking with him the administrators, official documents, food and provisions, and the funds of the department. DuRoy and Lindet reported this victory and the submission of Evreux to the Convention and to the Committee of Public Safety in dispatches during the next three days.[85] Lindet wrote from Pacy on July 14 to the Convention: ". . . The City of Evreux is entirely free; the rebels are fleeing, and retreating to Calvados . . . The Army of the Republic has conquered a department for liberty and the Constitution, and this victory has cost no blood; it will be more solid and enduring than conquests by devastation. An aide-de-camp will speak to the Convention of the events which have occurred up to this day. This faithful recital will interest the friends of humanity." Manuel, the aide-de-camp, gave this detailed report to the Convention on July 19, with these opening words: "Reason is the most powerful arm in the hands of free men."[86]

DuRoy and Lindet in a despatch to the Convention on July 17, wrote: "The rebels have been expelled from the Eure; but the center of the revolt is in Caen. It is necessary to extinguish this center." They recommended that the army that had liberated the

83. Aulard, *Recueil*, V, 244–5.
84. Montier, *Robert Lindet, op. cit.*, pp. 119, 128.
85. Aulard, *Recueil*, V, 260–1, 266; Arch. Nat. A. F. 11, 46, dossier 361.
86. *Moniteur*, XVII, 159–160.

Eure be sent to Calvados as an "army of pacifiers . . . Accelerate the expedition to Calvados to extinguish the center of the conspiracy."[87] The Convention accepted this recommendation on July 18, and extended the powers of Lindet, DuRoy and Bonnet de Meautruy (deputy from Calvados) to include Calvados and neighboring departments, and authorized them to "take all measures necessary to reestablish order, seize the conspirators, and assure the triumph of liberty."[88]

Citizens of the Eure rejoiced in the speedy and bloodless defeat of the federalist uprising. Bernay had remained loyal to the Convention throughout this insurrection. The municipal Council of Evreux "distinguished itself by noisy manifestations of joy . . . On Sunday, July 21, the new Constitution was proclaimed. On Thursday, the 23rd, Lindet announced, on the proposal of Hérault-Sechelles, that, to celebrate the return of liberty to the city of Evreux, the Convention had decided that six young, virtuous women, to whom the Republic would give a dowry of 2400 livres, would be united in wedlock with six young men chosen from the most worthy by an assembly of old men . . . At this news the joy became frenzy. On July 27, a tree of liberty was planted, with dancing, in the Saint-Léger Square. After this ceremony, *hélas* the effigy of Buzot . . . was committed to the ignominious flames. His home, condemned by the Convention to be razed, was demolished, stone by stone . . . Lindet, however, arrested only one person . . . This was, for the moment, the only reprisal of the victors."[89]

Gardembas, a contemporary friend of Buzot, judged the results of this pacification in Evreux and in the Eure: "Evreux was regenerated. All the citizens, pervaded by true repentance, showed only the most ardent wish to find the opportunity to atone for their error. The Representatives Robert Lindet, Duvoy [sic] and Bonnet left Evreux without having exercised any other act of severity than the provisional arrest of the Citizen Pain. The Representatives left for Lisieux, carrying with them the regrets and

87. Aulard, *Recueil*, V, 293–4.
88. *Moniteur*, XVII, 172.
89. L. Boivin-Champeaux, *Notices pour servir à l'Histoire de la Révolution* (Evreux: A. Huet), pp. 67–68.

the blessings of a commune they had liberated from oppression and reconquered for true liberty."[90]

Lindet and Bonnet informed the Committee of Public Safety from Evreux on July 29 that the Representatives on Mission Romme and Prieur had been released from imprisonment in Caen.[91] This had been announced to them by a conciliatory delegation from the Department of Calvados, urging the Representatives to speed their journey to Caen, where Wimpfen was in retreat and Buzot had fled. The departmental and commune officials were vying with each other in the retraction of their defection. The special representatives invited to Lisieux met with the constituted authorities and the popular society in the Cathedral there on July 30, in a conciliatory mood. They remained in Lisieux until August 3 when they went to Caen, preceded by a day by the army of pacification.

Early in August the Convention decreed the suppression of the *Société des Carabots* in Calvados, a society which had been the popular instrument of the insurrectionary Central Assembly. Lindet advised caution in rehabilitating the administrators who had so recently retracted their disloyalty, proposing new elections by the primary assemblies. He recommended excluding from office those who had retracted after July 15, and that those retracting before that date should only be reelected if the [special] representatives were convinced of their *civisme*. The other representatives favored less severe measures. Lindet asked the Committee of Public Safety to be relieved of his mission and be replaced by someone "very active, very vigilant, firm without harshness, who does not reveal his plans before the moment of execution. We persist in believing that the retractions are not a sufficient reason to keep weak or lax officials in their posts: the people do not believe in these retractions or they fear that they are not sincere."[92]

DuRoy, too, requested the Committee of Public Safety to recall him, on August 9, saying that his presence was useless.

90. M. Gaudet, *Mémoires sur la Révolution Française, par Buzot, précédés d'un précis de sa vie et des recherches historiques sur les Girondins* (Paris: Chez Bechet ainé, 1823), p. 247.

91. Aulard, *Recueil*, V, 417.

92. Montier, *Robert Lindet, op. cit.*, pp. 170–1.

Bonnet, in a letter to the Committee on the same day, referred
to these requests of the two representatives, attributing them to a
"little quarrel and a moment of temper which I witnessed yesterday. I had no idea they would take sides so hastily. This is why
you should act, in my judgment, wisely in paying no attention
to their requests. Lindet is a little difficult. He has a nervous
and sensitive manner and does not take remonstrances easily. He
is, however, a great worker and very capable. It would be a great
misfortune if he were replaced at the very moment when he is
au courant of this region."[93] The Convention and the Committee
declined to recall the two special representatives.

The harvest of 1793 was abundant in Calvados but there was
a shortage of wheat and bread because the greediness of the
farmers caused a rise in prices. They refused to cut the grain and
take it to market; the cities lacked bread. Lindet wrote to the
Committee of Public Safety on August 7: "Caen is without subsistence: can you get some for us? . . . Nothing is more pressing;
the security of the city depends on this." The three representatives
took measures to see that the grain was harvested. Lindet addressed a message to the people: ". . . The produce of the earth
is intended for the sustenance of all the people; whoever conceals
these products, monopolizes them, or refuses or delays putting
them on sale, is guilty of oppression of the social body; those
who are pledged to protect their properties have the right to life;
only in case of necessity is every citizen bound to give up his
property for public use, on receipt of an indemnity; only for the
most urgent reasons should one give up produce to the most
pressing needs of society, on payment of an indemnity, or on
payment of their true value."[94] This appeal and an order of
August 7 resulted in grain reappearing on the markets. The three
Representatives then concerned themselves with the recovery of
horses, harness and military equipment, purloined by the insurgents. Thus was Lindet having first hand experience with the
mammoth problems of subsistence that he was to face in the
Committee of Public Safety.

The Special Representatives proclaimed on August 18 the

93. Aulard, *Recueil*, V, 516–517.
94. Montier, *Robert Lindet, op. cit.*, pp. 173–4.

restoration of order in Caen and planted a tree to fraternity. Concord, however, did not prevail among the three. Lindet wrote to the Committee on August 27 to report on forty-five suspects, insurrectionists and thieves of national funds who should be arrested and tried. His two colleagues opposed this action and Lindet criticized them: "After what happened yesterday I would fail in my duty, if I did not inform you that my colleague [DuRoy] is not qualified to fulfill his mission . . . He does not wish to subscribe against Chatry, member of the insurrectionary Committee and editor of the *Journal du Calvados*. He consents to sign everything I wish against the citizens of *la Manche* but he wants me to leave to him his relatives and his friends in Caen . . . I should tell you that DuRoy and Bonnet are in no condition to fulfill a mission which requires amenity, decorum, severity, firmness and a great impartiality. Both have friends here." He quoted Bonnet as saying "If I subscribe to your point of view, my wife will not see me. Both have several times received members of the Directory of the Department who are the objects of accusation. I do not fear to saddle myself with public hatred . . . But do not count on the arrest of the guilty so long as DuRoy and Bonnet are here . . . You know how much it has cost me to write to you what you are now reading. The *état-major* can attest to my opinions."

Lindet and Bonnet sent a detailed report on supplies and subsistences to the Committee on August 29, stating that the Law of the Maximum was not being observed. "It is necessary to enforce the maximum and oblige all the departments to conform to the law of May 4. It is necessary that the law enlighten the people, and confound, astonish and smite the evil minded rich. You must make a prompt decision; there is not a moment to lose; while the rich calculate and feel nothing, the poor lose their way and hasten to their ruin . . . It is more pressing to pronounce strongly and immediately on this great question than on that of arming the citizens. The armament required by the most imperious necessity will be fatal if you delay for several days to pronounce this judgment between nature and wealth." What Lindet was really saying on the eve of the *levée en masse* was: "nourish first the people, arm them afterwards." The Convention decreed the Maximum for wheat for all France on September 4.

In a despatch to the Committee on September 1 Lindet accused Bonnet of misappropriating funds for his own use from a sum of 15,000 livres entrusted to him the year before by the minister of the interior for transmission to the hospital in Caen, but which he had transmitted in installments. The Convention recalled Bonnet and DuRoy on September 3 and sent Charles-François Oudot to join Lindet.[95] Le Carpentier (Manche) joined them from the Manche where he had been on mission. These representatives supervised the *levée en masse* of August 23 in Calvados and the Eure and also directed the establishment of public instruction in Caen. Lindet established the *Journal de l'Armée des côtes de Cherbourg* which continued to November 5. This journal ran summaries of the meetings of the popular societies, patriotic articles, and regulations and orders. Lindet and Oudot ordered the arrest of Simon, a coiner of false assignats, and his accomplices, on October 8.

Barère, for the Committee of Public Safety, on October 19, informed Lindet and Oudot that they could return to Paris as soon as they were relieved by Laplanche.[96] The Committee, over the signature of Carnot and Billaud-Varenne, wrote urgently to Lindet on October 27: "The multiplied tasks of the Committee require more than ever that you return to our midst. We recall you immediately, begging you to leave without delay and without awaiting him who is to replace you. Your colleague Oudot can remain at his post until the arrival of your successor." This was followed by an even more urgent summons from the Committee on October 31, in which for the first time Lindet was addressed by the intimate *tutoyer*. "There are tasks of the very highest importance, which we keenly want to see under your direction and special jurisdiction. For another reason, the Committee is reduced to five members by the special Commissions it has been obliged to assign elsewhere to its members. We await thee with the greatest eagerness; the public welfare will truly suffer by a longer delay in your arrival." Lindet replied that he was leaving but

95. Aulard, *Recueil*, VI, pp. 135–7, 174–6, 211, 223, 254–5.
96. *Ibid.*, VII, 502–3.

would stop for twenty-four hours in Bernay for a much needed rest.[97]

Lindet's biographer comments that Lindet had preserved his freedom of action on this important mission to the Eure and Calvados by neither giving nor attending soirées or festivals, but "living isolated and concentrating all his strength and faculties on the object of his mission. Work was his life."[98] Davy remarks that even the compromised insurgents were the objects of his kindness and protection, and that he never delivered them to the tribunals.[99] One of the persons whom he protected in Calvados was a M. Mesnil in Caen. Later, when Lindet needed an asylum, Mesnil concealed him in his house. Finally, when his security was assured, he married the daughter of his benefactor. Barère in his *Mémoires* wrote that Lindet "extinguished with a courageous prudence (sagesse) the firebrand of civil war lighted in the Eure and Calvados."[100]

During the time Lindet was in Calvados and the Eure, Marat was assassinated on July 13, the financial situation remained acute, food shortage was grave, a law against profiteers was decreed on July 26, and radical social proposals were being widely proclaimed by Roux, Varlet, and the Hébertists who had taken over the social program of the Enragés. The Committee of Public Safety on August 12 suggested a *levée en masse* to the Convention. Two days later, Carnot and Prieur (de la Côte d'Or), both engineering officers, were added to the Committee. The actual decree of the *levée en masse,* with its profound and far-reaching consequences, was voted on August 23.

Robert Lindet returned at this critical juncture to the Convention and the Committee of Public Safety with the kind of "grass roots" experience that was to stand him in good stead as he faced the herculean tasks that were soon to be delegated to him.

97. *Ibid.*, VIII, pp. 60, 146–7, 150.
98. Montier, *Robert Lindet, op. cit.*, 211–2.
99. Davy, *Les Conventionnels, op. cit.*, pp. 419–420.
100. B. Barère, *Mémoires*, publiés par Hippolyte Carnot et David (d'Angers) (Paris: Jules Labitte, 1842), I, 245.

CHAPTER FOUR

Robert Lindet's Role in the Committee of Public Safety—1793-1794

LINDET RETURNED TO PARIS when the dictatorship of the Committee of Public Safety was taking form. The tempo of the Revolution accelerated rapidly from August 10, to the "Constitution of the Terror" on December 4, which codified and consolidated the supreme power of the Committee. Lindet's own role was to be important and essential, though unobtrusive.

Affairs at home and abroad were more critical than ever. A long drought in the summer had reduced the harvest: peasants and shopkeepers were hoarding grain and food supplies, and prices rose. Military fortunes were at a low ebb, with the Austrians and Prussians advancing. The *sans-culottes* in the forty-eight Sections in Paris were increasingly unruly and susceptible to the radical agitation of the Enragés. Robespierre had been added to the Committee of Public Safety on July 17, to restore strong Montagnard leadership after the departure of Danton on July 10.

The Fête of August 10, of delegates from the primary assemblies throughout France and the Parisian masses, to celebrate the first anniversary of the Republic was a great success. At its climax, the new Constitution—recently approved by 1,801,918 for, to 11,610 against, but with only about one-fourth of the qualified voters voting—was solemnly placed on the national altar in the Champ-de-Mars.

The *levée en masse*, proposed on August 14 and decreed on the 23rd to "thunderous applause," created the "nation in arms." Barère, in presenting the proposal for the Committee, declared:

"The French people proclaims . . . that it rises *en masse* for the defense of its independence, its liberty, its constitution, in order to deliver its territory from the despots and their satellites." He described the Republic as a great besieged city, compelling France to become a vast armed camp.

Since Robert Lindet was to be closely associated with Carnot and Prieur (de la Côte-d'Or) in the defense of France, the main provisions of the *levée* should be summarized.[1] Conscription was to be complete and universal—of men, women, and production. The extraordinary production of arms was to be centered in Paris. Deputies, named by the Convention as Representatives on Mission, were to supervise production in their respective districts and were "invested with the unlimited powers attributed to the representatives of the people with the Armies [the first representatives on mission]. "By this "stupendous, awe-inspiring decree, the Committee laid the foundations for total war."[2] Republicanism and popular nationalism, as well as militarism—phenomena of the nineteenth and twentieth centuries—were implicit in the "nation in arms."

Excitement associated with the *levée*, the grave military situation, and food shortages impelled the Commune, Sections, and workers of Paris to mass pressure on the Convention, starting on September 4, seeking numerous extreme measures. In response to mob invasion of the Convention hall, concessions were promised and the slogan of the Commune, "Make terror the order of the day" was sanctioned. The Convention added two Hébertists, Billaud-Varenne and Collot d'Herbois, to the Committee of Public Safety, to strengthen the ties with the Commune and the Sections and to curb their fanatical radicalism with responsibility.

The growing dictatorship of the Committee advanced rapidly during September and October by legislation giving it power to appoint all committees of the Convention, including its great rival, the Committee of General Security, which it proceeded at once to purge and fill with uncompromising terrorists; by incorporating the Jacobin Clubs into the governmental system, empowering them to denounce suspects and unworthy officials; by the Law of Suspects

1. Stewart, *A Documentary Survey, op. cit.*, pp. 472–4.
2. Gershoy, *Bertrand Barère, op. cit.*, p. 178.

of September 17, with its greatly-increased powers of arrest and detention; by the inclusive Law of the Maximum of September 29; and by the Subsistence Commission established by decree on October 22. Robert Lindet was to be the person most responsible for the execution of these last two decrees.

The Convention on October 10, after Robespierre had summarized the alarming events of the preceding three months, decreed that the "provisional government of France is revolutionary until the peace." This decree spelled out the declaration of September 5, and served as the basis of government until the "Constitution of the Terror" on December 4 codified into a single document the previous decrees, thus completing the structure of the emergency dictatorship of the Committee of Public Safety. The ministers were directly responsible to the Committee. Representatives on Mission, chosen by the Committee and confirmed by the Convention, were to supervise the conscription of men and horses, keep the armies in the field efficient and their officers faithful and loyal, and report every ten days to the Committee. The departments were shorn of much of their authority, to the advantage of the more revolutionary districts and municipalities.

Thus was created the "octopus-like revolutionary government, focused in the Committee of Public Safety, working through the Committee of General Security and the Revolutionary Tribunal and thrusting its tentacles out into the departments through the representatives on mission, the Revolutionary army and revolutionary committees."[3] It was a war government, a "dictatorship of distress," highly centralized, and consciously and ruthlessly using terror against foreign and domestic foes of the Republic and the Revolution.

Robespierre said at the time of its establishment: "The mainspring of popular government in a revolution is at once virtue and terror; virtue without which terror is baleful, terror without which virtue is powerless." By virtue the revolutionaries meant "love of the patrie, the sacrifice of personal interests to the state, the quasi-mystical absorption of the individual will into the general will."[4]

3. Louis R. Gottschalk, *The Era of the French Revolution* (Cambridge: Houghton Mifflin Co., 1929), p. 243.
4. Gershoy, *The French Revolution, op. cit.*, p. 273.

While the Government of the Terror was taking shape, under the guiding hand of Carnot, military fortunes began to turn for the better. Ineffective generals were replaced by able and ambitious young generals—Jourdan, Pichegru and Hoche. The first important victory of the Revolution was won at Wattignies by the Army of the North under Jourdan on October 16, with Carnot collaborating in person. The guillotine began its deadly work at this time. During October, Marie Antoinette, the Duke of Orleans, thirty-one Girondins, Madame Roland, Bailly, and Barnave were beheaded. Seventy-three deputies who had protested the purge of the Girondins, May 31-June 2, were imprisoned. The executions spread into the departments and terror became the order of the day.

Robert Lindet had been recalled from his mission in Calvados and the Eure at the end of October, to assume an important responsibility in the dictatorship of the Great Committee in the government of the Terror, "revolutionary to the peace." He had missed the tumultuous days of September and October in the capital, though he had witnessed their milder counterparts in the two departments.

The dynamo of the revolutionary power house had become the Committee of Public Safety. It exercised a collective dictatorship —"collegial" might be a more modern term. It was more informal than a modern cabinet but, in the crisis, it practiced effective unity and solidarity. Gershoy writes: "There was nothing in all Europe to match the concentrated power of the new leviathan, nothing to compare with the quick flow of command from the vital center to the outlying parts of the immense administrative bureaucracy."[5] Marcel Reinhard says the dictatorship "encompassed the total national life."[6]

The crisis the twelve men on the Committee faced is put dramatically by Professor Palmer: "Anarchy within, invasion from without. A country cracking from outside pressure, disintegrating from internal strain. Revolution at its height. War. Inflation. Hunger. Fear. Hate. Sabotage. Fantastic hopes. Boundless ideal-

5. *Bertrand Barère, op. cit.*, pp. 198–9.
6. Marcel Reinhard, *Le Grand Carnot, L'Organisateur de la Victoire, 1792–1823* (Paris: Hachette, 1952), II, p. 56.

ism. And the horrible knowledge, for the men in power, that if they failed they would die as criminals, murderers of their king. And the dread that all the gains of the Revolution would be lost. And the faith that if they won they would bring Liberty, Equality and Fraternity into the world."[7]

To a considerable degree the Great Committee met this crisis successfully. With no pre-Revolutionary experience in government and with no pre-Revolutionary ideology, strategy and tactics worked out for a Revolution such as Lenin had done by 1917, they improvised ably in defending and consolidating the Revolution. They raised the "nation in arms" and organized and inspired it to save France and the Revolution. They governed France strongly and effectively, using the instrument of the Terror to combat counter-revolution and civil war and to consolidate the Revolution until they turned it to partisan purposes. They bred the inevitable revulsion and reaction of 9 Thermidor and thereafter, and thus conditioned the conservative, weak bourgeois republic of the Directory.

It was the Committee of September, 1793, that was *the* government of revolutionary France for nearly a year, to July 27, 1794 (Thermidor). Two of the members, Jean-Bon Saint-André and Prieur (de la Marne) were usually on mission to the armies. The nine who were the most active in Paris until 9 Thermidor were Barère, Billaud-Varenne, Carnot, Collot d'Herbois, Couthon, Robert Lindet, Prieur (de la Côte-d'Or), Robespierre, and Saint-Just. There were eight lawyers, two army officers, one actor-playwright, and one Protestant pastor (a former sea captain). Their average age was just over thirty-seven. The oldest was Robert Lindet, forty-seven; Carnot was forty; Robespierre was thirty-five and Saint-Just was the youngest at twenty-six. All were of the middle class excepting Hérault, a noble. All but Collot d'Herbois were relatively well to do and Hérault was wealthy. All were heirs of the philosophy of the eighteenth century. They were radical revolutionaries. Their sincerity and devotion were beyond question. They were scrupulously honest and remained above every consideration of personal profit, devoting single-minded and tremendous energy to the great tasks of war government.

7. *Twelve Who Ruled, op. cit.,* p. 5.

The Committee of Public Safety gradually organized itself into specialties in the fall of 1793, and within these the responsible members were essentially their own masters, their colleagues usually approving without discussion those proposals that did not touch matters of general political concern. Carnot, Lindet and Prieur (de la Côte-d'Or) occupied themselves with military affairs. Carnot had as his special function the personnel and the tactical direction of the armies. Prieur was charged with the manufacture of arms and munitions, and the hospital service. Lindet was responsible for subsistence, clothing, transportation, the administration and enforcement of the Maximum, and much of the work usually assumed by a minister of the interior. Professor Gershoy says these three "hardworking experts were apolitical."[8]

The "indefatigable" Barère, a facile, conciliatory speaker and a thorough parliamentarian, usually reported to the Convention for the Committee, and served as its chief liaison officer with the Convention. Barère and Hérault directed foreign affairs. Barère, Collot d'Herbois and Couthon were entrusted with correspondence with the officials and with representatives on mission. The honest and conscientious Saint-André directed the "miserable" navy, and was much of the time on mission. Couthon, of the twisted legs, the noble brow, the "bell-like" voice, and with the revolutionary spirit of a fanatic, gave himself to politics and the police. He was a devoted follower of Robespierre. Saint-Just spent about half his time on mission, particularly to the armies, a work in which he was eminently successful. He also devoted himself to constitutional legislation. Robespierre, virtuous, "self-righteous and introverted" disciple of Rousseau, gave some particular attention to public instruction but mixed freely in most matters, especially in foreign affairs, usually in a large, general fashion without attention to technical knowledge or to the practical application of details. He served as a sort of "front" for the Committee, whose members used his popularity to get their measures adopted.

There is some evidence that public opinion of the day classified the nine most active members of the Committee into three groups, named by their contemporaries as the revolutionaries, the *poli-*

8. *Bertrand Barère, op. cit.*, p. 202.

tiques, and the workers.[9] The first group according to this point of view, included Barère, Billaud-Varenne and Collot d'Herbois. Their reports were particularly designed to arouse the political emotions. The second group, Robespierre, Couthon and Saint-Just, prepared the legislative program, and controlled the police and the revolutionary tribunal. The third group was composed of Carnot, Lindet and Prieur (de la Côte-d'Or). Modern scholars dispute this classification. While they admit the special functions and responsibilities of the individual members, they unite them in responsibility, not necessarily equal, for public and political policy. Certainly it is hardly fair not to call all of the members "workers" for all worked with feverish activity.

One is astounded at the variety of problems resolved by the Committee, at the multitude of orders and decrees ground out daily in the political and administrative mill, and at the quantity of letters comprising the official correspondence of the members. These men were not trained administrators, nor were most of them of the bureaucratic type, nor did they have the benefit of the whole paraphernalia of modern government and business. The methods of executing the will of the Committee strike a modern as confused, cumbersome and inefficient. Much of the clerical work was done laboriously by hand, of course, by the members themselves, or was delegated to the considerable number of persons attached to the Committee and to the ministers. The National Archives attest, however, to the tremendous amount of work contributed by each member to the conduct of government.

Members of the Great Committee often worked fifteen to sixteen hours a day. Their offices were in the Tuileries, the old royal palace. They were assisted by numerous functionaries, clerks, secretaries, couriers, and specialists. They were besieged by army officers, politicians and contractors. They were usually in their offices by eight in the morning. The first of their two daily meetings came around ten o'clock—an informal meeting for those who

9. Hippolyte Carnot, *Mémoires sur Carnot Par Son Fils* (Paris: Paguerre, Libraire-Editeur, 1861–1863), I, pp. 347–8; Lacretelle, jeune (Charles-Joseph), *Précis Historique de la Révolution Française, Convention Nationale* (Paris: De l'Imprimerie de Didot Jeune, 1803), I, pp. 141–2; H. Taine, *Les Origines de la France Contemporaine—La Révolution* (Paris: Hachette et Cie., 1885), III, pp. 234–244.

could take the time to attend. It took place in the sumptuous Salle de Diane in the Pavillon de Flor, in the light green room, around the large oval table with its green cloth, loaded with inkwells and piles of papers and documents. About noon, when the Convention convened, some of the members, usually Barère and Couthon, walked across the Tuileries Gardens to the Convention. Most of the members remained busily engaged in their offices. They dined in the early evening in nearby restaurants and were back at work at seven.

They met at ten in the evening for the important general conference in the "green room" behind closed and closely-guarded doors. These sessions often lasted to well after midnight and sometimes even all night. No one presided, and no minutes of these policy-making meetings were kept; their secrecy was hardly ever violated by leaks of any kind. The discussions must have been vigorous and oftentimes passionate. All members were dedicated to the Revolution and when decisions were reached they were presented as collective decisions. Resolutions were adopted to be presented to the Convention for its ratification, orders were written, instructions were drafted for those on mission, and proclamations issued. When the meetings ran into the early morning hours some of the members snatched a few hours of sleep on cots in their offices.

Decisions were made in these evening meetings on the responsibility of the Committee as a whole. For these it seems that at least three signatures were necessary, while the signature of a single member was sufficient to validate a decree of the Convention, and many of the orders and decrees of the Committee have but one or two signatures. Carnot, who attended the majority of the Committee's meetings and was a signer of most of its orders and decrees, once spoke of the necessity of giving between five and six hundred signatures a day, many of which he said were given without reading and "as of confidence," by which he meant blanket approval of the actions of the member within his particular competency.

In a study of 608 orders of the Committee for the short period of May 20-June 18, 1794, Robert Lindet headed the list of "presumptive" authors with 207, of which 183 were for supply and transport. Most of these were written by him personally. Carnot was second with 177, of which 130 had to do with the army and navy. Then came Prieur (de la Côte-d'Or) with 157, of which 114 had to do with munitions. Robespierre had eight.[10]

Lindet worked tirelessly in his office. He was probably better prepared for administrative work than his colleagues and his talents were decidedly of that nature. How did he work and what were his relations with his associates? Prieur (de la Côte-d'Or), with whom he was closely associated, gives a clear picture: "Lindet, absorbed in continuous work, kept himself with his numerous staff, in a separate location. He attended the Committee meetings only for matters relating to his own special province . . . A well-informed lawyer and already aged [sic: he was forty-seven!], he was a man of unquestioned integrity and a great worker. He was always to be found, pen in hand, in his offices, where he spent from twelve to fifteen hours daily. Cold in manner to his colleagues, with some of whom he had amicable relations, he gave himself, however, obligingly to their operations when they had need of help from his office. Isolated in his functions, he came to the meetings of the Committee only to report on important measures, or to seek support for those that needed the full force of the government behind them. The ensemble of his office was very considerable."[11] Amand Montier reports that Lindet's "principle was never to postpone until the morrow what could be done today."[12] Hippolyte Carnot writes that his father, Lazare, was only fully in accord with Prieur (de la Côte-d'Or) in the Committee, and while he recognized the merit and services of Lindet, the latter did not "inspire in him any personal sympathy."[13]

---

10. Palmer, *Twelve Who Ruled, op. cit.*, p. 402. Professor Palmer quotes a study by J. M. Thompson of the special responsibilities of the members in an earlier period of the four months after September 23, 1793. Of the 920 documents issued in that period, Carnot penned or first signed 272, Barère 244, Prieur (de la Côte-d'Or) 146, Lindet 91, Robespierre 77, Collot 29, Saint-Just 12, Prieur (de la Marne) one. *Ibid.*, p. 109.

11. George Bouchard, *Prieur de la Côte-d'Or, membre du Comité de Salut Public: un organisateur de la victoire* (Paris: Librairie Historique R. Clavreuil, 1946), pp. 437, 448.

12. *Robert Lindet, op. cit.*, p. 215.

13. *Mémoires sur Carnot, op. cit.*, I, p. 510.

Lindet, despite the economic liberalism which he shared with most of his colleagues on the Committee and in the Convention, was the person most responsible for the administration and enforcement of the Law of the Maximum, and for the directed, planned economy that the exigencies of the internal and external crisis, and popular pressure, compelled.

The Old Regime had, of course, enforced strict regulations of, and government intervention in, the economy under prevailing mercantilist doctrines and practices. Mercantilism was designed more for the enhancement of State power and wealth than the welfare of the people, or the interests of the bourgeoisie. Price-fixing was sometimes resorted to, particularly for foodstuffs, in times of bad harvests.[14]

Mercantilism was increasingly challenged by the bourgeoisie, disciples of the Physiocrats, the Economists, and greatly influenced by Turgot. They believed in natural laws of property and wealth, in free trade and unlimited competition. The State was to respect these laws and interfere and intervene as little as possible. *Laissez faire, laissez passer!*[15]

The great majority of the *Cahiers de doléances* of 1789 demanded the continuation of government regulations. The National Assembly, however, dominated by the great landowners and the bourgeoisie, did not accept this popular mandate. The Declaration of Rights of Man and the Citizen declared property to be a sacred and inviolable right. All restrictions on trade were abolished. In the Convention, the Mountain opposed the fixing of prices for commodities, advocated by the Enragés. It had to surrender, however, by adopting the first Law of the Maximum on May 4, which fixed prices on grains. This limited and poorly-enforced law proved inadequate. The decree of July 26 against profiteers and hoarding, and the decree of August 9, establishing state granaries (*greniers d'abondance*) in each district, designed to calm the agitators and avoid a general maximum, were never more than

14. Jacques Ellul, *Histoire des Institutions de l'Epoque Franque à la Révolution* (Paris: Presses Universitaires, 1962), p. 446, and for an excellent summary of mercantilism in the section on "L'Etatisme economique."

15. See Albert Mathiez, *La Vie Chère et le mouvement social sous la Terreur* (Paris: Payot, 1927), passim.

"paper expedients." Finally, on September 29, under pressure from the Hébertists and the Commune the Convention adopted the definitive Law of the Maximum.

Robert Lindet and Bonnet, just a month previously on August 29, had expressed themselves on the Maximum, from Caen: "The price of grains has not been fixed in the department of Ille-et-Vilaine. The law of May 4 has not been executed." For instance, cultivators in the district of Avranches, where the maximum was enforced, took their grain to the markets of Ille-et-Vilaine and sold a sack for 110 livres, when the maximum in their district was 55 livres. "One can imagine the spirit of rivalry and jealousy that exists between the towns and the countryside . . . One cannot ignore the fact that the cultivators desire the repeal of the law of the maximum, but one can be sure that if the unlimited freedom to sell grain at will is granted, the price will triple before three months . . . This tripling . . . will bring ruin to a part of the people . . . When the claims of wealth are in opposition to the rights of man, it is necessary to restrain the former."[16]

Albert Mathiez comments that in these words lay the "germ of the class policy which will impose itself more and more in the Convention . . . This necessity was obvious at the beginning to a person of the worth of Robert Lindet, but it was not seen at once by the other representatives."[17]

The Law of the Maximum that Lindet was to administer was extensive and detailed. It fixed a uniform price for all of France for cereals, flour, forage, tobacco, salt and soap. Other commodities and goods of prime necessity were to have their prices fixed by the district authorities at a rate one-third higher than the average price in 1790. No allowances were made for the cost of transportation, and the rate of profit was not legally fixed. Persons disobeying the law were subject to a fine and were to be entered on the list of suspects. Farmers had to declare their harvest and merchants the inventory of their stock to the district administrations, which were empowered to inflict severe penalties on all violators of the law. All exports of essential merchandise and commodities were prohibited.

16. Aulard, *Recueil*, VI, 174–176.
17. *La Vie Chère, op. cit.*, p. 386.

For wages, the Maximum set the rate at half again as much as the rate of 1790. The fixed rate of wages was to be established by the municipalities, whereas the rate on commodities fell within the sphere of the district authorities. Workmen refusing to work at the official wages were to be "impressed" by the municipalities and punished by three days imprisonment.[18]

On the motion of Saint-Just the Convention on October 10, decreed that a census of all cereals be taken. The country was to be divided into zones for the purposes of provisioning. Paris was to be provisioned for a year from its own special area. Resistance was to be crushed by the central revolutionary army, detachments of which would be quartered on the recalcitrant communes at the expense of the rich. In Paris the Commune controlled the distribution of cards for rationing bread, meat, sugar and soap; it empowered the commissaries for food speculators to make domiciliary visits, even in private homes. Most towns in France followed the Paris model.

An amending decree to the Maximum, of November 1, provided for the increase of prices at the point of production by one-third over the price of June 1790, plus a rate per league for transportation, plus five percent for the wholesaler and ten percent for the retailer. The law affected thirty-nine commodities of general consumption, but did not include firewood, fish, tobacco, salt, milk, and poultry. The increase for wages was also fixed at fifty percent over the rates prevailing in June 1790.[19]

Thus the "economic dictatorship" of the Terror as finally completed included government requisitioning for the armies at the official maximum, municipal or district requisitioning to feed the civilian population, using a system of bread and meat ration cards and a uniform *pain d'égalité*, the closing of the stock exchange,

18. Professor Rudé reports that an inquiry in June 1793 revealed that prices in the country as a whole for essential commodities had doubled or even trebled since 1790, and in the same period, wages had likewise risen by 100 to 150 percent according to region. *op. cit.*, p. 129.

19. The Law of September 29, as thus amended, arrested inflation. The assignats had twenty-two percent of their nominal value in August 1793. This had risen to thirty-three percent in November and to forty-eight percent in December. Rudé, *op. cit.*, p. 130.

and government supervision and control of foreign trade and foreign exchange.[20]

Lindet worked particularly through the Subsistence Commission in administering the Law of the Maximum. The Convention established this Commission, on motion of the Committee of Public Safety, on October 22, to execute the Law, with the widest powers in controlling the war-time economy. The Committee named Lindet to be its liaison with the Commission and to supervise its activities. It was given supreme control, not only over agricultural and industrial production, but also over mines, coal and lumber. It could requisition food supplies, with the right of seizure if need be, and it had full control over transportation.

The three Commissioners named to the Commission were Brunet, administrator of the Department of Herault, Goujon, *procureur général syndic* of the Department of Seine-et-Oise, and Raisson, secretary-general of the Department of Paris. The first secretary-general of the Commission was Tissot, brother-in-law of Goujon. The Commission was installed at first in rooms in the Ministry of the Interior but soon took over the Hôtel de Toulouse, the home of an émigré, in the rue de la Vuilliere. It had a staff of over 500 officials and clerks. Its work was divided into three major areas: resources and statistics; distribution and requisition; accounts and bookkeeping. The Commission developed a program of education and propaganda to increase production. It sent the *Feuille de Cultivateur* in 2,000 free copies to clubs, districts, and prominent cultivators and distributed the *Journal des Arts et*

20. The administration and effectiveness, or ineffectiveness, of the Law of the Maximum are ably treated in the following volumes: Marcel Marion, *Histoire Financière de la France depuis 1715*, Tome III, 1792–1797, 2me éd. (Paris: Rousseau et Cie., 1927); Georges Lefebvre, *Les Paysans du Nord Pendant la Révolution Française* (Bari: Editori Laterza, 1959), particularly Ch. VIII, "Le Maximum et les Paysans," which is detailed and excellent; Georges Lefebvre, *Etudes Orléanaises*. Volume I, *Contributions à l'Etude des Structures Sociales* à la fin du XVIIIe Siècle; Volume II, *Subsistances et Maximum* (1789-An IV). (*Mémoires et Documents*, Vol. XV). (Paris: Centre National de la Recherche Scientifique, 1962, 1963). These admirable volumes are both economic and social. The second volume, particularly, deals with the sans-culottes and their support of the Maximum, and their relations with the *Montagnards* who under normal circumstances were attached to the principles of private property and to liberal economics.

Manufactures to the industrialists. It also circulated generous excerpts from Arthur Young's writings on agriculture.

The Commission assigned a definite area to each army in which to provision itself until the Commission could work out a system of requisitioning under its direct control. It sent agents throughout France and through them began a mammoth census of the national food supply. It commandeered boats and wagons for the transportation of goods and it centralized the maintenance of roads and canals. The Commission had the power to draft workers for government service in the nationalized munitions factories and could invoke the death sentence against any who interfered with the drafting of workers in greater Paris, where most of the factories were concentrated. Municipalities were empowered to assign citizens to the farms of mobilized soldiers and to other lands needing laborers. Prisoners of war and deserters were assigned to public works, particularly on roads and canals. Soldiers in garrison were requisitioned to help in the harvests. In November the Commission was given the monopoly over the import trade and in December the power to authorize exports. The corvée was legalized in January.

The Navigation Act of September 21 had declared commercial war on England and had closed France to all export and import trade with the enemy. On December 10 the Commission was authorized to import prime commodities and materials from allied and neutral nations. French merchants had already been permitted to export luxury goods. The Great Committee authorized the export of specie to pay for imported grains and other necessities.[21]

Lindet gave himself without stint to his special responsibilities, particularly those associated with the Subsistence Commission. The paucity of detailed reports of deliberations in the Commission make it difficult to reconstruct actual procedures but certain records are illustrative. The session of November 5, 1793, for instance, was reported as follows: "The session opened at six in the evening. Citizens Robert Lindet and Prieur, representatives of

21. See Georges Lefebvre, *Études sur la Révolution Française* (Paris: Presses Universitaires de France, 1954), "Le Commerce Extérieur en l'an II," pp. 170–198.

the people, Pache, mayor of Paris, Hassenfratz, Monge, Citizen Gautier, deputy of the minister of war, and the administrators of army subsistence met with the Commissioners . . ."[22] Three nights later the same persons met from seven to eleven-thirty. So the record went.

The Commission was authorized by the Committee of Public Safety on November 22, on the former's proposal, to import grain from the United States, up to five millions. Lindet wrote the order —signed also by Barère, C.-A. Prieur, Carnot, Robespierre, and Billaud-Varenne—authorizing the French legation in the United States to facilitate these purchases by crediting them to the debt of the United States to France.[23]

At the Commission's session on December 29 the orders from the Committees of Public Safety, General Security, and Finance were read, naming Citizens Cambon, Dupuis, Lindet, Moyse Bayle, and Dubarran as representatives to work with the Commission to execute the requisition of industries and other properties of bankers and capitalists. When it was proposed in the Commission's session of February 6, 1794, that a new commission on imports and exports be established, it was reported that "Citizen Lindet seemed to be impressed by the idea."[24] On March 1, with Lindet and Pache present, the discussion was on provisioning civilian Paris, the army in the capital, and the armies in the field. Lindet spoke at length and with the result that "the observations of Citizen Lindet appeared to overcome the objections, leaving no difficulties excepting the choice of means."[25]

Lindet also had close relations with the Committee of Agriculture and Commerce.[26] Decrees of the Convention in February and March 1794 established a Commission of Transports under his direction. This anticipated the reorganization provided for by the

22. Pierre Caron, *La Commission des Subsistances de l'An II* (Paris: Librairie Leroux, 1925), p. 9. Hassenfratz and Monge were leading scientists.

23. Aulard, *Recueil*, VIII, 618–9.

24. Caron, *La Commission, op. cit.*, pp. xvi, 323.

25. Aulard, *Recueil*, VIII, 429–430.

26. *Procès-Verbaux des Comités d'Agriculture et de Commerce de la Constituante, de la Législative et de la Convention*, publiées et annotés par Fernand Gerbeaux et Charles Schmidt (Paris: Imprimerie Nationale, 1908), Tome III, Tome IV (1910), passim.

decree of April 1, which abolished the Executive Council and the six ministries, replacing them by twelve commissions controlled by the Committee of Public Safety. Lindet was also active in the Commissions of Agriculture and the Arts, Commerce, and Provisions. After Thermidor, on October 12, 1794, the Convention elected three members to the Committee of Commerce and Supplies, to complete its membership. The three were Lindet, Morisson, and Borel. The Committee chose Lindet as its president. He also regularly attended the weekly meetings of the War Committee of the Convention, on Saturday evenings at eight o'clock, along with Carnot and Prieur (de la Côte-d'Or).[27]

The National Archives silently but eloquently attest to the industry of Robert Lindet in these critical days. Hundreds, even thousands, of orders, usually having to do with supplies, were written by him and signed by other colleagues on the Great Committee. Many were signed only by him. Some of these were on the recommendations of the Commission of Transports, Mails and Stage-Coaches. Great numbers had to do with relatively minor matters. An order, for instance, of the Subsistence Commission of April 18, 1794, countersigned as approved by Saint-Just and Lindet, dealt with the requisition of the wines and liquors of émigrés, condemned and detained persons. Another, more important, of April 25, 1794, by the Committee of Public Safety, on recommendation of the Commission of Commerce and Supplies, authorized the evaluation by experts of jewels and precious stones belonging to the nation. They were to be shipped by Citizens Perrin and Cablas of Marseilles, to Constantinople and elsewhere for sale, on a two percent commission, up to one million, plus their expenses, or two percent on one to three millions, but without expenses.[28]

While the Committee of Public Safety was grappling with urgent problems during the fall and in the early winter of 1793, the anti-Christian, anti-Catholic movement ran its course under the leadership of the Hébertists. Churches were sacked, relics were desecrated, and the riches of the churches were poured into the national treasury. Great numbers of priests—including Gobel, bishop of

27. Reinhard, *Le Grand Carnot, op. cit.*, II, p. 63.
28. These orders are found in Arch. Nat'l. A. F. 11, 20, dossier 144.

Paris, and Thomas Lindet, bishop of Evreux—unfrocked themselves in public ceremonies. This de-christianization movement was climaxed in the Festival of Reason on November 10 in Notre Dame, transformed into a Temple of Reason. A religion of the Revolution was substituted for Catholic Christianity, with the *Patrie*—with its patriotic saints and martyrs—substituted for God. The name of the Supreme Being was always carefully mentioned, with Reason usually given as one of his principal attributes.[29]

The Convention and the Committee of Public Safety—most of whose members were deists—for political reasons, did not officially associate themselves with this anti-religious movement. Robespierre, alone, strongly opposed the de-christianization campaign, both for religious and political reasons. Although he favored a revolutionary religion, his religious temperament was shocked by the excesses of the movement. He had scant respect for its leaders, and he saw its harmful effects on the revolution at home and on foreign policy. The European monarchs, in fact, responded to the movement with a vigorous manifesto. Robespierre persuaded the Jacobin Club, in a powerful speech on November 21, to purge the principal leaders, and on December 8 he persuaded the Convention to decree complete freedom of worship. The more enduring result of anti-religious feeling was the revolutionary calendar adopted by decrees of October 5, 24, and November 24, which dated the French Era from the Republic on September 22, 1792.

Robert Lindet was probably too busy to be involved in this anti-christian interlude. In the conduct of his special responsibilities he found it necessary to prevent the arrest of Paris bankers and use them in the service of the state. He had to oppose Robespierre who suspected their *civisme* and wished them liquidated. The biographer of Prieur (de la Côte-d'Or) comments that on this

29. Albert Soboul, "Sentiment Religeux et Cultes Populaires Pendant la Révolution-Saintes: patriotiques et martyrs de la liberté." *Extrait de Archives de Sociologie des Religions*, Juillet-Décembre, 1956, No. 2, pp. 73–87. (Clermont-Ferrand, G. de Bussac, 1956). Soboul thinks that Aulard and Mathiez, though recognizing the religious character of the revolutionary cults, had not penetrated deeply enough, and from somewhat false perspectives, namely, the "political preoccupation of Aulard or the sociological deformation of Mathiez." Soboul admits that the absence of documentary material makes it difficult to do anything but raise problems and suggest certain guidelines.

occasion "Lindet revealed again an enlightened zeal sustained by great courage."[30]

During the Terror Lindet intervened in some instances to protect suspects of whose guilt there was considerable doubt. One such instance is described in stark detail by Otto Wolff. It involved 132 citizens of Nantes despatched by Jean-Baptiste Carrier to the Revolutionary Tribunal at five o'clock in the morning of November 27, 1793. Wolff describes their long journey: "Chained together in pairs, they had been driven out of the town without seeing their families to walk the long road from Nantes to Paris in all kinds of weather. Dragged from gaol to gaol, they finally ended up on the rotten palliasses of the Conciergerie. 'Prison sickness' took its toll, the bucket which had to serve their most primitive needs polluted such air as there was and their diseased bodies were weakened still further by the inadequate and often uneatable food. Before the tribunal had even seen them their number had been reduced from 132 to eighty-four."

These unfortunates had a friend from Nantes who interceded on their behalf, a precocious youth of twenty-three who had just arrived in Paris. Gabriel Julien Ouvrard, the son of a paper mill owner in Brittany, at nineteen had accumulated 300,000 francs through speculation in paper at the beginning of the Revolution. He had gone into the wholesale grocery business in Nantes. Some of his business friends, no doubt, were among the suspects from Nantes. Unable to reach or bribe Fouquier-Tinville, Ouvrard, by guile, through the Duplay sisters, interviewed Robespierre in their home. This intercession was fruitless. Then an approach to Fouquier-Tinville through a beautiful young woman was successful and the prisoners were transferred from the Conciergerie, usually the final stage to the guillotine.

Wolff continues: "The man to whom the Committee of Public Safety looked for concrete evidence against the prisoners was Robert Lindet, the financial expert of the Revolution and a man with a highly developed sense of justice. He deliberately took so long to provide any evidence at all that by the time the prisoners came up for trial Robespierre had fallen and they were acquitted. It is virtually certain that Ouvrard was partly responsible for the

30. Bouchard, *op. cit.*, p. 449.

fact that the evidence produced was favourable." Ouvrard then pursued the matter which had brought him to Paris, namely, to secure compensation for the loss of his father's paper mill, burned during the fighting in the Vendée. The Committee of Public Safety, on the basis of a report by Lindet, approved an indemnity of 200,000 francs.[31]

Lindet also became involved during these winter months in the exercise of the Terror in the Eure. After the "farcical" end of the Federalist uprising in Normandy and Brittany with the defeat of the insurrectionary forces at Pacy-sur-Eure, there was little trouble in the Eure.[32] Lindet intervened vigorously in the case of the arrested municipal officers of the town of Conches. To ferret out suspects three Representatives on Mission had been sent into the west by decrees of the Convention on August 23–24, 1793— Legendre, Lacroix and Louchet. After working in Evreux they went to Conches, a town rumored to be the center of dissension on November 28. In 1792 two popular societies had existed there, one composed of moderates who opposed the establishment of a republic, the other the *Amis de la Montagne,* whose leaders wanted to expel the moderate town officers. After investigation, the representatives ordered the arrest of the eight municipal officers and their transfer to Paris to go before the Revolutionary Tribunal. Eulalie Savarre of Conches, and François, her cousin in Paris, approached Lindet to intercede. Lindet informed Fouquier-Tinville that he would appear before the Revolutionary Tribunal on their behalf, asking to be informed of the time of the hearing. He also sent the Committee of General Security a memorandum in their favor, which he also had printed and distributed.[33] The accused

31. Otto Wolff, translated by Steward Thomson, *Ouvrard, Speculator of Genius, 1770–1846* (London: Barrie and Rockliff, 1962), pp. 24–27. cf. Montier, *Robert Lindet, op. cit.,* pp. 238–9.

32. Donald Greer, *The Incidence of the Terror During the French Revolution* (Cambridge: Harvard University Press, 1935), pp. 143; 149; 163. In fact, the Criminal Tribunal of Evreux imposed only four death sentences in the Department between May, 1793 and July, 1794. Two were of the working class for counter-revolutionary opinions, and two for the refractory clergy.

33. This episode is related fully in M. L. Boivin-Champeaux, *Les Fédéralistes du Département de l'Eure devant le Tribunal Révolutionnaire, 1793– 1794* (Rouen: Imprimerie de E. Cagniard, 1865). See Montier, *Robert Lindet, op. cit.,* Ch. XIII.

were notified of their accusation on January 10, 1794, and informed that they were to appear for trial on January 16. Fouquier-Tinville failed to notify Lindet. The trial, in fact, was held earlier than scheduled and the eight were condemned to die. Learning of this, Lindet appeared and, supported by Carnot and Barère, had the proceedings suspended. He demanded the right to speak before the Tribunal, reminding it of his forthcoming report on the federalist conspiracy. He said that he had been instrumental in quelling the mild uprising in the Eure on his earlier mission, and that Conches had been but a tiny link in the uprising. He begged the Tribunal to await the vote of the Convention on the general matter. The Public Prosecutor commented that the guilt of the eight had been legally proven and that the jury had been adequately informed. Lindet insisted, however, and because of his membership on the Committee of Public Safety, the Tribunal sent back the accusations.

At a joint session of the two great Committees that evening Lindet reported what had happened during the day. Justifying his position, he recalled his mission to the west and his policy of conciliation. A policy of vengeance now would cause new troubles, would revive the Norman insurrection, and raise up a new Charlotte Corday in Eulalie Savarre. "We have enlightened the departments, we have not conquered them." During the long session Robespierre was silent. It was finally decided to give the Public Prosecutor an oral order to suspend the process until further notice. The next day Lindet so informed Fouquier-Tinville and the accused were returned to the Conciergerie. The terrorists then turned their wrath upon the Parisian François Savarre, who ultimately was guillotined.

Legendre took the tribune in the Convention on February 7 to pursue the accusation against the eight, attacking Lindet as their defender. The latter was absent at the time, but, informed by his brother Thomas, entered the hall and mounted the tribune. He explained his appearance before the Revolutionary Tribunal and before the two great Committees. Whatever mistakes had been made by these municipal officers were to be imputed to inexperience, to weakness and to error. These were not crimes to be punished by death. "A gloomy silence suddenly fell over the Convention. His eyes ranged the benches of the assembly, seeking his colleagues on the Committees, and meeting only the pale and glacial look of Robespierre, who, impassive, did not cease to stare at him. Enslaved and trembling, the Convention only awaited to strike for a sign from the tyrant . . . It was Danton who interposed, Danton, worn out by controversies and proscriptions, who advocated, too late, the return of humane laws and the rapprochement of the parties." Danton proposed that Lacroix, Legendre and Lindet together make a general report. Lindet gave a sign of assent. The debate was closed and the Convention voted a decree which may perhaps be "considered as the last evidence of union of the diverse factions of the Mountain."[34] The process against the officers of Conches remained indefinitely suspended. They were finally liberated in the aftermath of 9 Thermidor.[35]

During these months, Lindet had served as the "great intendant for civilian France and for the armies,"[36] performing "almost daily, one doesn't know how, the miracle of the multiplication of bread."[37] With Carnot and Prieur (de la Côte-d'Or), he was truly an "organizer of victory."

The Revolution now moved into the fateful months of Ventôse and Thermidor.

34. Boivin-Champeaux, *op. cit.*, pp. 18, 20, 21.
35. Robert Lindet's lengthy reply to Legendre and his exposition of his policies as a Representative to put down rebellion in the Eure, is reported in the *Moniteur*, XIX, pp. 421–3, session of February 7, 1794.
36. Montier, *Robert Lindet, op. cit.*, p. 231.
37. Davy, *Les Conventionnels de l'Eure, op. cit.*, pp. 428–9.

CHAPTER FIVE

9 Thermidor and the Thermidorian Reaction

THE FACTIONAL CRISIS that culminated in the spring of 1794 with the execution, first of the Hébertists, and then of Danton and his associates, had begun in earnest in the previous December. The dramatic climax in the struggle for power came on July 27–28 —known as 9 Thermidor—with the execution of Robespierre and his most devoted followers.

The Hébertists—also known as Ultras, or extremists—were a small group of men who controlled the Paris Commune, the Cordelier Club, and the War Ministry. They included Hébert, Vincent, Momoro, Ronsin, Bouchotte, Fouché, Carrier, Anacharsis Clootz and a few other foreign refugees and adventurers. The Hébertists were champions of the lower bourgeoisie and the poor and were violently anti-Catholic. Hébert edited the vigorous journal, *Père Duchesne*, which had great influence in the Sections and a wide circulation elsewhere. Hébert was also substitute *procureur* to Chaumette, who as *procureur* was head of the municipal council. Robespierre detested Hébert, believing him to be an atheist and probably a communalist. Chaumette was a sincere, puritanical young man of thirty-one, devoted to the interests of the people, and with a deep compassion for the poor. These extremists favored war to the bitter end, overthrow of all monarchies, and repression of all suspects.

At the other end of the continuum were the Moderates—also called Citras—led by Danton, with Desmoulins as his ardent lieutenant. They favored a policy of moderation, relaxation of

119

severity, "dilution of proletarianism," conclusion of peace with the European Powers, and the establishment of their kind of bourgeois government. The two leaders were handicapped by some unsavory associates who were in bad odor at the Jacobins.

Desmoulins launched the *Vieux Cordelier* on December 5, 1793, dedicating the first numbers to Danton and Robespierre, and attacking the Hébertists. The sheet achieved an immediate success, particularly among those fearing the continuation of the regime of severity, including a number of aristocrats, speculators, profiteers, and royalists. The issue of December 15 vigorously attacked the Hébertists, and the feud began between Desmoulins and Hébert in their respective journals. Robespierre approved the attacks made in the first two numbers of the *Vieux Cordelier* but thereafter pleaded for moderation. When this did not happen he began to distrust Danton and Desmoulins and turned on both the Hébertists and Moderates. In the third number of his journal Desmoulins initiated a "great public campaign to end the regime of Terror," writing: "Let a regime of love replace the regime of Terror."[1] Robespierre had not seen this number before its release.

Influenced by this issue, people began urging the release of suspects under arrest. Robespierre voted for the establishment of a Clemency Commission, but on December 25, gave an address "On the principles of Revolutionary Government," in which he said: "We must crush both the internal and foreign enemies of the Republic or perish with it . . . Terror is merely justice, prompt, severe, and inflexible." The speech intensified the factional strife, which now moved into the Jacobin and Cordelier Clubs. Billaud-Varenne was already calling for Danton's head. Collot d'Herbois severely censured Danton's corrupt friend, Philippeaux, in the Jacobins on January 5, although treating Desmoulins gently. Robespierre, though calling on the Jacobins to rally behind the Committee of Public Safety on January 7, on the following day denounced Fabre d'Eglantine, intimate friend of Danton, for duplicity and corruption. Fabre was expelled from the Club, as was Desmoulins two days later. The Cordeliers in turn expelled Fabre, Philippeaux, Bourdon, and Desmoulins, having vainly tried to persuade the latter to change the name of his journal. Arrests,

1. Gershoy, *Barère, op cit.*, p. 204.

releases, and counter-arrests of Hébertists and Dantonists followed.

Robespierre eloquently addressed the Convention, in the name of the Great Committee, on February 5, on the state of the nation, in what Palmer calls the "most memorable of his addresses . . . Not only the best expression of Robespierre's real ideas, but also one of the most notable utterances in the history of democracy."[2]

The Report was directed against the policy of moderation, blaming the national ills and dangers on the machinations of the coalition and castigating Danton's peace proposals as defeatism. "We have laid before you in all its purity," spoke Robespierre, "the moral and political principles of popular government . . . The only citizens in the Republic are the republicans." A republic so conceived must remain at war with its own counter-revolutionaries and at war with Europe. The revolutionary government existed to win the war and establish a democratic constitutional government, of which the chief danger was internal faction. Shortly after this speech Robespierre became ill and was absent from affairs for more than a month, during which Saint-Just and Collot d'Herbois, strong-willed antagonists, faced each other in the Convention.

Lindet and the Subsistence Commission were working during these three months on new schedules of the Maximum, which were presented to the Convention on February 21, and adopted after lengthy discussion and some opposition. The new schedules of prices, permitting a higher mark-up on goods, were printed in a document of 1,278 pages, and distributed in the districts.[3]

Economic crisis, hunger, and popular discontent aggravated the factional battle. The food shortage was particularly acute in Paris. Bread was scarce, no meat was to be had, vegetables, butter, fruit,

2. *Twelve Who Ruled, op. cit.*, pp. 272, 273. The speech is given in *Moniteur*, XIX, 401–408, under the title: "Report on the principles of political morality which should guide the National convention in the internal administration of the Republic."

3. *Moniteur*, XIX, 526 ff. See Henry E. Bourne, "Maximum Prices in France in 1793 and 1794," *American Historical Review*, XXIII (1917), pp. 107–113; Henry E. Bourne, "Food Control and Price-fixing in Revolutionary France," *Journal of Political Economy*, XXVII (1919), pp. 73–94, 188–209; Rudé, *op. cit.*, passim; Marc Bouloiseau, *Le Comité de Salut Public* (1793–1795), (Paris: Presses Universitaires de France, 1962), Ch. VIII, "L'Economie Dirigée et la Politique Sociale."

eggs, and fish were almost non-existent, coal and wood were in short supply and the cost was exorbitant. Black market selling of controlled commodities flourished. The underfed *sans-culottes* fixed responsibility and blame on the government. "Disorder," writes Professor Palmer, "was spreading among the workers in the manufacture of arms. On the morning of 16 Ventôse—March 6—a placard fastened at the door of one of the government shops was found defaced. It was a statement of regulations concerning hours, signed by six members of the Committee of Public Safety. Under Barère's name was scrawled *cannibal*. Under those of Lindet and C.-A. Prieur, who had the most direct charge of the economic regime, was written *cheaters of the people, foolish and stupid as it always is*—and also in red crayon, *robbers, murderers*."[4]

The famous "laws of Ventôse"—February 26, March 3, 6 and 13—decreed, among other matters, the confiscation of property of convicted suspects and distribution to "indigent patriots," though this was soon amended to provide for supplementary sales as nationalized property. Suspects—enemies of the Republic— were to be imprisoned until the peace and then banished for life. The Committee of General Security, on its own authority, was to release patriots wrongfully imprisoned, which meant that 300,000 persons were to be investigated.[5]

The defense of the *patrie* during the factional struggle claimed the single-minded attention of the men most responsible for it. Lindet, in his accustomed role, on March 13 defended the order to requisition merchandise for exportation in an address to the Convention: "You do not doubt your right to requisition twelve hundred thousand men, exposed to death every day in fighting your enemies; I believe, for the same reasons and for the most convincing motives, one has the right to requisition goods destined for export in order to procure supplies and materials which are indisputably necessary to clothe, nourish, arm and sustain the 1,200,000 citizens whom you send to face dangers and cement your liberty with their blood! You have no other means of payments abroad."[6]

4. *Twelve Who Ruled, op cit.*, p. 253; see Rudé, *op. cit.*, pp. 128–136.
5. *Moniteur*, XIX, 565–9; 611; 632–3; 686–692.
6. Montier, *op. cit.*, p. 229.

The Cordelier Club was now the center of the attack on the Moderates, capitalizing on the distress of the *sans-culottes*. Hébert addressed the members on February 20: "Increase the revolutionary army [in Paris], let it march with the guillotine in front and I will guarantee abundance." Placards appeared in the congested quarters on March 1, urging the people to dissolve the Convention and replace it by a dictator who would restore prosperity. Unruly soldiers threatened to free imprisoned patriots and destroy counter-revolutionaries, whom they accused the Convention of protecting.

The call of Hébert and the Cordeliers for an insurrection on March 4 was, however, cooly received by the Commune and Sections. Lindet had fortuitously granted two million livres to the Commune to provide food for the city and thus quiet the mass partisans of the Hébertists. The Committee of Public Safety took prompt action by decrees to investigate the Cordeliers and arrest the conspirators. Robespierre—recovered from his illness —and others thundered against the Hébertist "conspiracy" in the Jacobins on March 14, to the warm applause of the members and the citizens in the galleries.[7]

Saint-Just formally attacked the extremist factions in the Convention on March 13, in a long, rambling speech, accusing them of being tools of the Coalition and involved in the "foreign conspiracy."[8] The Convention immediately named certain large categories of persons as traitors. Hébert, Ronsin, Vincent, Momoro, Manuel and others were arrested at once. Clootz and a few others were included to give credence to the fiction of the foreign conspiracy. Twenty in all were arrested and all but Laboureau—who was acquitted—were condemned on March 20, as accomplices of Pitt and Coburg, and executed four days later.

The two Revolutionary Committees on March 17 ordered the

7. F.-A. Aulard, *La Société des Jacobins: Recueil de Documents* (Paris: Librairie Léopold Cerf, etc., 1895), V, pp. 681, 683. For speeches by Couthon and Robespierre on March 16, and by Robespierre and Tallien on March 17, *Ibid.*, pp. 692–5, 696–7.

8. *Moniteur*, XX, 17–20. The revealing title of his accusation is: "Report on the factions of foreign inspiration, and on the conspiracy plotted by them in the French Republic, to destroy representative government, and starve Paris."

arrest of Chaumette, who had had nothing to do with the plans for the Hébertist insurrection. Lindet and Couthon, present at the session, did not sign the order. Saint-Just informed the Convention on that day that Hérault-Sechelles and his friend, Simond, had been arrested. Lindet and Prieur (de la Côte-d'Or), though present, did not sign the order. The Convention dissolved the revolutionary army in Paris, closed the Cordelier Club and the popular clubs in the Sections, appointed Fleuriot and Payan, partisans of Robespierre, to the places of Pache and Chaumette at the Hôtel de Ville, and retained Hanriot—devoted to Robespierre—as commander of the National Guards.

Aristocrats and royalists rejoiced in what they interpreted as a conservative turn in the Revolution. The Convention was overwhelmed by congratulations for its prompt action against the Hébertists, but the Committee of Public Safety was alarmed by the fact that the Moderates were exultant. Robespierre and Saint-Just, in their attacks in the Convention and in the Jacobins, had been careful to assess guilt equally between both Hébertists and Moderates.

The Jacobins immediately shifted their attack to the Moderates, demanding Danton's head, and gradually wearing down Robespierre's resistance. Mutual friends brought the two men together, hoping for a reconciliation, but the meeting was fruitless and only increased their differences. The unsavoury East India Company scandal, involving Fabre, and Chabot's group, being officially aired at the time, was used to implicate and smear Danton. Not only did the two strong revolutionaries oppose each other, but, as Professor Kerr puts it: "Two different worlds; Robespierre stood for the Puritan sansculotte Republic and the strict enforcement of justice, while Danton, loose and easy-going toward offenses even against himself, stood for the lax bourgeois Republic which triumphed in Thermidor."[9]

The show-down in the struggle for power came rapidly. The two great Committees prepared for the destruction of the Moderates during the week of March 23–30. It was decided to include Desmoulins with Danton, Philippeaux and Delacroix, and associate them all with the notorious Chabot group, implicating them further

9. Wilfred B. Kerr, *The Reign of Terror* (Toronto: University of Toronto Press, 1927), p. 352.

in the so-called conspiracy sponsored by the Coalition. Saint-Just and Robespierre presented the report to a full and turbulent session of the two Committees on March 30.

Lindet opposed the arrests. There is some evidence that at first Carnot stood with him though he finally signed the order. In refusing to sign, Lindet declared: "I am here to supply the citizens, not to kill patriots." Rhul also refused to sign because of his friendship for Danton. Robespierre was the last to sign. The arrests were made at once and the victims incarcerated. Paris was stunned by the sensational arrests.

No time was lost. The Convention assembled at eleven the next morning, with Tallien presiding. Legendre's courageous proposal that Danton appear and speak on his own behalf was defeated by the influence of Robespierre's arrival in the hall. Saint-Just presented the long accusation: "Report on the conspiracy plotted to secure a change of dynasty," in an assembly in which profound silence reigned.[10] "The revolution is in the people and no longer in the renown of certain personalities . . . There is something terrible in the sacred love of the *patrie*: it is so exclusive that it sacrifices everything without pity . . . Your Committees . . . have charged me to demand justice of you . . . against those who for a long time have betrayed the popular cause . . . I thus denounce the last partisans of royalism, those who for five years have served the factions and have pursued liberty only as a tiger pursues its prey . . ."

Saint-Just gave a long bill of particulars in chronological order from 1789, outlining the internal conspiracy with its alleged foreign counterparts. He called Hébert a "covert partisan of royalty," and Fabre an accomplice of Danton and a "royalist all the time in the depths of his heart, [who] dissimulated like the others because he was cowardly." Desmoulins was first a dupe, then an accomplice and instrument of Danton and Fabre. After summarizing his version of Danton's conduct during the Revolution, Saint-Just thundered: "Danton, you have served tyranny . . . Danton, you were the accomplice of Mirabeau, of Orleans, of Dumouriez, of Brissot . . . Evil citizen, you have conspired . . ."

The decree, ordering the trial of the accused, along with Fabre

10. *Moniteur*, **XX**, 97–104.

d'Eglantine, for having been "implicated in the conspiracy designed to restore the monarchy and destroy the national representation and the republican government," was adopted unanimously and with great applause. Couthon reported the events of the day immediately to the Jacobin Club, at great length and in roseate colors: "Finally, the political horizon clears up, the sky becomes serene, and the friends of the Republic can breathe again. The Convention, like the armies, advances to the charge . . ."[11]

The trial, which was public, began on April 2 in the Revolutionary Tribunal. Fifteen persons were on trial, including the usual sprinkling of foreigners. When Desmoulins was asked his age he replied, "I have the same age as the *sansculotte* Jesus, thirty-three years." Danton, when asked his age and domicile, answered, "my dwelling will soon be in nothingness; as to my name, you will find it in the pantheon of history."[12] On the second day of the trial Danton spoke powerfully in his own defense. He asked that sixteen members of the Convention, including Lindet, be called as witnesses. The judges and the public accuser acceded to the request and sent a message to the Tuileries, asking the Great Committee what they should do. The Committee denied Danton's request, the "docile" Convention ordered the prisoners to be silenced, and the defense was summarily ended.

The trial was a mere formality, consisting mainly of short questions and answers, with no witnesses and virtually no documentary evidence. Sentence of death came speedily. On April 5 the executioner Sanson led the victims to the guillotine while David nonchalantly sketched them from the terrace of an adjoining cafe. Danton's shaggy head was the last to fall into the basket, just as the compassionate curtain of darkness fell. The Convention had given a stunned submission to the Committee of Public Safety. Robespierre was supreme, dominating the Jacobins and the Revolutionary Tribunal, but less powerful in the two Committees.

Four days prior to the executions, the Convention consummated the centralization of absolute power in the Committee of Public Safety by unanimously approving the abolition of the six ministries and the provisional Executive Council, replacing them by twelve

11. Aulard, *Jacobins, op. cit.*, VI, pp. 33–36.
12. *Moniteur*, XX, 128.

commissions to be apointed by the Great Committee. Details of administration only were to be entrusted to the commissions. The twelve were civil administration, police and the courts of justice, education, agriculture and the arts, commerce and provisions, public works, public relief, transport, finance, army and navy, munitions, and foreign relations. Each commission was supervised by a member of the Great Committee. Lindet's major, very natural, assignment, was the Commission of Commerce and Provisions.[13]

Carnot, in presenting the proposal to the Convention from the Great Committee, pointed out that the ministries were an institution created by the kings to perpetuate hereditary government, maintain the three Orders, and preserve distinctions and prejudices. They were "incompatible with the republican regime." He described the Great Committee as a "direct emanation, an integral and responsible" part of the Convention, to which should be delegated "all those tasks of a secondary importance that cannot be discussed in the general assembly." This revolutionary organization would prevail until a "solid peace" made it possible to change the methods that crime, the factions, and the late convulsions of the aristocracy had forced on the Convention.

The consequent fundamental reorganization of administration, even at the time of the executions of the Dantonists, was effected smoothly. Lindet commented on this later when he called attention to "how well those responsible had been able to organize all branches of the government without suspending public services, and how this prodigious change had produced no other effect than the acceleration and success of all civil and military operations."[14]

Waging war and governing the country had to go on, of course, in these tumultuous days. Lindet's success in provisioning the armies was attested to by Cambon, who reported on March 22 that during the past five months the cost of the upkeep of the army was only half of what it had been for the same period the year before when the army had numbered only one-third its present size. "Lindet, working all day and every day, created competence out of chaos, and succeeded in winning from the

13. *Moniteur*, XX, 111–112; 114–117.
14. Quoted in Hippolyte Carnot, *Mémoires sur Carnot, op. cit.*, I, pp. 353–4.

generals, not wont to be overly generous in such matters, a reputation second only to that of Carnot as an organizer of victory."[15]
The two, naturally, worked in close liaison with each other. Lindet
reported in fact: "Carnot informed me of the movements of the
armies, the needs of the troops; I transmitted the orders of the
Committee to the proper Commissions, I sent them the plans, the
means of execution, and I pointed out the resources; each night I
summarized and accounted for the operations of the day, and
planned the work and operations of the next day with the Commissions."[16]

Robespierre, with the Hébertists and Dantonists out of the way,
began to establish the politico-religious system he had in mind as a
distinctive religion of liberty, equality and humanity, with its utopian reign of Virtue and Justice. The deist Carnot was president
of the Convention on May 7 when Robespierre made his proposal,
to prolonged applause. There were to be two positive tenets of
faith in the new civic religion: belief in the Supreme Being, and
belief in the immortality of the soul. Robespierre said: "The real
priest of the Supreme Being is nature; his worship virtue; his
ceremonies, the joy of a great people assembled, under his eyes,
to draw tighter the sweet bonds of universal fraternity and to
present to him the homage of sensitive and pure hearts." There
were to be thirty-six annual festivals on the *décadis*. Especially
to be commemorated were January 21, when the "tyrant was
beheaded," May 31, when the Girondins were expelled, August
10, when the monarchy was overthrown, and, greatest of all,
July 14, when the Bastille was stormed. There was to be no priesthood. Hymns and chants were to be composed to "inculcate
patriotic and republican virtues in the minds of the regenerated
people." The inscription "Temple of Reason," wherever it appeared, was to be replaced by "To the Supreme Being."[17]

The inaugural Fête of the Supreme Being was held on June 8,
dramatically staged and directed by David, artist-member of the
Convention. Robespierre, president of the Convention at the time,

15. J. M. Thompson, *The French Revolution* (Oxford: Basil Blackwell,
1955), p. 426.
16. Montier, *op. cit.*, pp. 225–6.
17. *Moniteur*, XX, 403–411; Stewart, *op. cit.*, pp. 526–8.

mounted an outdoor tribune in the Tuileries and delivered an ardent "sermon" as a devout disciple of Rousseau. He then led a great procession to the Champs de Mars where he climbed an artificial mountain to the chanting of a hymn especially composed by André Chenier. Robespierre was blissfully happy.[18]

He at once turned to the completion of the structure of the Terror. Two days after the Fête of the Supreme Being he pushed through the decree of June 10—known as the Law of 22 Prairial —in the face of some opposition.[19] All forms of evidence were to be permissible, and when there was material evidence, witnesses were dispensed with; public defenders were no longer to be provided; the right to denounce conspirators was accorded to all citizens and that of delivering prisoners to the Revolutionary Tribunal was extended to the two Committees, to the public prosecutor, to representatives on mission, and to the Convention; only one punishment, that of death, was to be meted out. The Revolutionary Tribunal was divided into four sections, each with its complement of president, judges, and jurors, sitting simultaneously, and steadily delivering judgments. "Justice" was to be done wholesale. "The new judicial system," writes Professor Gershoy, "that Robespierre had defended became the instrument of the monstrous 'Great Terror.' In the seven weeks between its enactment and the fall of Robespierre, the guillotine claimed more victims than it had in the preceding fourteen months . . . The Law of 22 Prairial was the catalyst of fears, old and new, in the Convention."[20]

Robespierre also availed himself of the Bureau of General Police of the Great Committee, which had been established on April 23, for police supervision of all state office-holders and for surveillance over public administration. The Robespierrists on the Committee—Robespierre, Saint-Just, Couthon—assumed the direction of the Bureau, usually in turn, assisted by a director—a friend of Saint-Just—two assistants and ten clerks. The Committee reorganized the Bureau on June 20, dividing it into four sections.

18. David Lloyd Dowd, *Pageant-Master of the Republic: Jacques-Louis David and the French Revolution* (Lincoln: University of Nebraska Studies, 1948), pp. 119–124.
19. Stewart, *op. cit.*, pp. 528–531.
20. Gershoy, *Barère, op. cit.*, p. 243.

The Terror became a veritable massacre after June 10. Executions in Paris had mounted steadily after the beheading of Danton on April 5. Between that date and June 10, 723 had been sent to the guillotine, while 288 were acquitted or "no case." But from June 10 to July 28—10 Thermidor—1,376 unfortunates were condemned and executed. Prior to this the majority of the executions had been in the provinces, particularly where counter-revolution was greatest or where the pressure on the frontiers was most intense. Fifty percent of all executions in Paris during the entire Terror occurred in these two months. The majority were from the upper classes.

The public was satiated with blood after the execution of Danton. The guillotine had to be moved two or three times in June and July because of the popular feeling of revulsion. Fear was universal. The Convention was nearly deserted. When Prieur was elected to the presidency only 117 were in attendance. Dissensions appeared in the Committee of Public Safety. Hitherto it had presented a united front in the Convention and to the public. The dictatorship was a collective one and Robespierre was generally regarded as its leader, since he usually defended its political policies in the Convention.[21]

Dissension within the Committee became "open war" after the middle of June. The arrest of Catherine Théot, a religious fanatic known as "Mother of God," on June 15 was a rebuff to her patron, Robespierre, and subjected him to ridicule. With difficulty he had the charges against her quashed. Hurt to the quick, he absented himself from the Committee and the Convention, only frequenting the Jacobin Club. He attended his own bureau to June 30, but only one meeting of the Committee before July 18.

Lindet's reaction to Robespierre was revealed during these days. When Robespierre walked out on the Great Committee he is reported to have cried, dramatically and incredulously: " 'Save the *patrie* without me!' 'The *patrie* is not a man,' Robert Lindet replied." Later, Lindet vigorously opposed the proposal of Saint-Just

21. Lefebvre, *Études, op cit.*, p. 72: "The dictatorship of the Committee was indisputably collective. Since it was Robespierre, however, who the most clearly and courageously defended the policy of the government, he came to be considered its chief."

and Le Bas to bestow the dictatorship on Robespierre, declaring in the Committee: "We have not made the Revolution for the profit of one man. Tell your master that I oppose this proposal," and he left the meeting.[22]

Collot d'Herbois and Billaud-Varenne were now openly opposing Robespierre in the Great Committee. The "feud" between Carnot and Saint-Just over the direction of the war effort tightened. Saint-Just, as early as January 21, had curtly criticized the military transport and supply system, for which Carnot, Prieur (de la Côte-d'Or) and Lindet were responsible.[23] Robespierre supported Saint-Just in his clash with Carnot, while Prieur naturally stood with Carnot. Mathiez writes that "Barère and Robert Lindet manoeuvred between the two groups, trying to reconcile them."[24]

Carnot in one of the heated and tense sessions of the Great Committee in late June or early July accused Saint-Just and his associates: "You are ridiculous dictators," and at another time, in the presence of Levasseur (de la Sarthe), he said to Robespierre: "You commit only arbitrary acts in your office of general police. You are a dictator."[25] Alphonse de Lamartine reports a strained meeting of the Great Committee shortly before July 27, in which Billaud-Varenne replied to some sally: "There are men who conceal their ambition under their youth, and play Alcibiades to become Pisistratus! At the name of Pisistratus, Robespierre thought himself alluded to. He desired to withdraw, but Robert Lindet prevented this with mild and wise advise."[26]

22. Montier, *op. cit.*, p. 247 footnote.

23. Geoffrey Bruun, *Saint-Just, Apostle of the Terror* (Boston: Houghton Mifflin Co., 1932), p. 85.

24. Albert Mathiez, *The Fall of Robespierre* (New York: Alfred A. Knopf, 1927), p. 145; Ch. VIII, "The Divisions in the Committees of Government on the Eve of 9 Thermidor." cf. Eugene N. Curtis, *Saint-Just* (New York: Columbia University Press, 1933), Chs. XVIII–XIX; Gershoy, *Barère, op. cit.*, pp. 256 ff; Palmer, *Twelve Who Ruled, op. cit.*, pp. 368 ff. It is interesting to note that nine-tenths of the orders issued by the Committee of Public Safety in May and June were drafted by Carnot, Prieur, and Lindet.

25. Ernest Hamel, *Histoire de Robespierre* (Paris: Chez l'Auteur, 1867), III, pp. 599–600.

26. Alphonse de Lamartine, *History of the Girondists-or Personal Memoir of the Patriots of the French Revolution* from unpublished sources (London: Henry G. Bohn, 1848), III, p. 487.

Turning to the war, Charleroi was captured by French arms on June 25, and the next day the important and decisive battle of Fleurus was won. There was less reason than ever, therefore, for the continuation of the Terror. The struggle in the great Committee, however, did not abate. The battle was fought in the two Committees, the Convention, and in the Jacobins.

Fouché and others spread rumours that the Great Committee was preparing extensive lists of proscriptions, including many Montagnards. Saint-Just spoke of the necessity for a dictatorship. Carnot foresightedly dispatched a large part of the Parisian artillery —friendly to the *sans-culottes*—to the front. Couthon hotly denounced this in the Jacobin Club, which responded by attacking Robespierre's enemies. In the Great Committee the majority of the members besought Robespierre and Saint-Just to have the Law of 22 Prairial—June 10—repealed. In the violent debate the two threatened to appeal to mass action. The Committee of General Security, almost in its entirety, now opposed Robespierre. The latter withdrew almost completely from the government and when he did attend meetings of the Committee, refused to sign orders, giving only five signatures to unimportant decrees between July 3–27. The attack on him in the Convention doubled—the members fearing for their own heads. On July 1, Robespierre in the Jacobin Club vigorously defended the continued use of reprisals and executions; and during July 19–28 the Revolutionary Tribunal gave 354 death sentences.[27]

Fouché and his associates began tentative negotiations with the right. The Jacobins, Commune, and Hanriot urged Robespierre to suppress his enemies by force, but he declined. A feeble effort at reconciliation in the Great Committee on July 23 failed. The next day, Robespierre repeated his allegations of a conspiracy in the Jacobins, and on the following day, the Club memorialized the Convention in such vague and large terms that the general alarm was intensified. Labor unrest and agitation came to a head on July 23, with the publication of the new wage rates prescribed by the

---

27. Arch. Nat'l. A. F. Carton 47, folder 368, for the names, with their occupations. A list of those liberated in the same period is also given.

Law of Maximum, reducing wages, even for those engaged in the manufacture of arms.

Robespierre addressed the Convention on July 26, in what was, on the whole, a vague and weak speech. He actually accused only Ramel and Mallarmé, but he left everyone uneasy. He treated his colleagues on the Great Committee lightly, although he attacked the conduct of the war—meaning Carnot—and the direction of the finances—meaning Cambon. "The counter-revolution," he said, "is in the administration of the finances."[28] He named the Cambons, Mallarmés, and Ramels as responsible. The conspiracy, he alleged, had even penetrated into the two Committees and had pitted the two against each other. For the first time a member of the Great Committee reproached his colleagues in the Convention. Finally, Robespierre offered his remedy to the "evil": punish the traitors, purge the Committee of General Security and renovate its staff; subordinate it to the Great Committee; purify the latter; restore the unity of government under the supreme authority of the National Convention and, thus, "crush all factions by the weight of the national authority, and build upon their ruins the power of justice and liberty."

Billaud-Varenne took the tribune for the opposition, proposing that the speech be referred to the Committee of Public Safety, saying: "I would rather my body serve as a footstool to an ambitious man than by my silence authorize his misdeeds." This was a challenge from the highest quarter in the government. Robespierre was asked to name the conspirators but he "evaded once more, made a general statement and lost the day."[29] The Jacobins, however, responded with loyal enthusiasm when Robespierre repeated the two-hour speech—with some changes—in the Club.[30] Billaud-Varenne and Collot d'Herbois were not only denied a hearing in the Jacobins, but were driven from the hall.

Saint-Just stayed on at the Committee of Public Safety, drafting a speech, while the other members were too paralyzed to do anything. Collot d'Herbois, coming from the Jacobins, denounced

28. Aulard, *Jacobins, op. cit.*, VI, p. 275.
29. Kerr, *The Reign of Terror, op. cit.*, p. 471.
30. Aulard, *Jacobins, op. cit.*, VI, pp. 246–281.

Saint-Just for preparing an accusation against his colleagues. The latter finally admitted as much and "turning upon Carnot with calm arrogance," added, "You are not forgotten either, and you will find that I have treated you in masterful fashion."[31]

The Convention convened at ten o'clock on July 27—the fateful day. Robespierre was dressed in the costume he had worn at the Fête of the Supreme Being. Saint-Just went directly to the Convention without submitting his speech to the Great Committee, as he had promised. He did not get far into his speech. Tallien interrupted him first, followed by Billaud-Varenne, who denounced Robespierre as a moderate. Robespierre's demand to speak was hooted down. Tallien's motion to arrest Robespierre's followers was adopted. Barère failed to calm the Convention. At last, Louchet, an obscure Montagnard and extreme terrorist, moved the arrest of Robespierre. Augustin Robespierre asked to be included with his brother. Le Bas offered himself, and Couthon and Saint-Just were included in the decree. Hanriot had been suspended earlier in the day as commander of the Paris Guard. The two Committees, later in the day, ordered the secret arrest—over the signatures of Dubarrau, Rhul, Barère, Carnot and Lindet—of the secretary of Saint-Just, who had made a "great disturbance on July 26 at the Jacobins."[32]

The action moved from the Convention to the city. Efforts of Payan, Fleuriot-Lescaut, mayor of Paris, and Hanriot—before his arrest—to rouse the Commune and the Sections to defend Robespierre and his followers failed, despite a protest assembly of workers demonstrating against the new wage scales. The workers were dissillusioned with Robespierre. During the night thirty-nine of the forty-eight Sections were in permanent session, with thirty-five supporting the Convention. Before morning all had gone over to the Convention.[33] Fleuriot signed a decree outlawing fourteen deputies, including Collot d'Herbois, Fréron, Tallien, Carnot, and Fouché.

Robespierre violated his detention, went to the Hôtel de Ville but took no action against the Convention. Hanriot was released at

31. Bruun, *Saint-Just, op. cit.*, p. 131.
32. Arch. Nat'l. A. F. Carton 47, folder 363.
33. Rudé, *The Crowd, op. cit.*, pp. 138–141.

eight-thirty but did not act. The Jacobins stood with the Commune. The Convention, in night session, declared Robespierre and his associates *hors la loi* and empowered Barras to lead the forces against the insurrection. Carnot had already ordered the young patriots in camp at Sablons to come, armed, to the Convention. Robespierre finally agreed to lead the insurrection but it was too late. The armed forces of the Commune in front of the Hôtel de Ville had disappeared by one-thirty in the morning of July 28, when Barras appeared with troops to face the mob. He surprised and arrested Robespierre, his associates and about forty members of the Commune. The paralytic Couthon fell in trying to flee, the younger Robespierre jumped out of a window, Le Bas shot himself, and Robespierre, who apparently tried to commit suicide and had had his jaw shattered by a bullet, was taken on a stretcher to the anteroom of the Great Committee, where his wounds were dressed.[34]

The outlaws were taken to a room in the Tuileries, adjoining the Convention hall. They needed only to be identified to be condemned. At four in the afternoon of July 28 the condemned leaders and their friends in the Commune—twenty-one in all—were driven to the guillotine. The first head to fall into the basket was that of Couthon, the last that of Robespierre.[35]

Lindet apparently did not take a leading part in the events of July 27–28, although he was associated with his five colleagues in signing all the orders issued by the majority of the members relating to the latest "conspiracy."[36] In addition to these, eight orders were signed by Lindet on July 27 dealing with commerce and provisions.[37]

Reorganization of the government was inaugurated immediately. Supreme power was withdrawn progressively from the Committee of Public Safety and restored to the National Convention. The Paris Commune was suppressed and the Parisian National Guard

34. Gershoy, *Barère, op. cit.*, p. 259.
35. See Palmer, *Twelve Who Ruled, op. cit.*, pp. 372–381, for a short, vivid description of the dramatic events of July 26–28. Robespierre's head fell 113 days after Danton's execution, and just a year after he had been added to the Great Committee.
36. Montier, *op. cit.*, pp. 249–250.
37. Aulard, *Recueil*, XV, 457–467.

reformed. It was decreed on July 29 that one-fourth of the Great Committee should retire each month and no retiring member could be re-elected until a month had elapsed. Two days later the Committee was reconstituted. The six new members were Eschassériaux, Thuriot, Tallien, Laloy, Bréard, and Treilhard. Barère, Lindet, Prieur (de la Côte-d'Or), Carnot, Billaud-Varenne, and Collot d'Herbois completed the twelve. The policy of the new Committee was to modify and moderate, but not to stop, the Terror, pursue the war, and maintain the revolutionary government, with a purged Jacobin Club, and a reformed Revolutionary Tribunal.

The Jacobin Club was re-opened on August 1, on motion of Legendre, despite Carnot's opposition. In the first week of August, 500 suspects were released in Paris and during the rest of the month 3,000 were freed. Fouquier-Tinville was impeached on August 2, and the Law of 22 Prairial was repealed. The powers of representatives on mission were curtailed by decrees in August. The executive powers hitherto monopolized by the two great Committees were distributed among the sixteen new committees which replaced the previous twenty-one. The Committee of Public Safety was restricted largely to foreign affairs and the direction of the war. The Convention was asserting itself as it never had before.

Billaud-Varenne and Collot d'Herbois left the Great Committee on September 1. Already under attack in the Thermidorian reaction, they were the first members to leave. On September 14, the 132 prisoners who had been turned over to the Revolutionary Tribunal in January by the bloodthirsty Carrier, were acquitted and the Nantes Tribunal was impeached. This alarmed Billaud-Varenne and Collot d'Herbois and they fulminated in the Jacobin Club. Shortly thereafter, on November 12, the Club was closed, and Carrier was tried and executed on December 16.

At the next monthly elections to the Committee of Public Safety, on October 6, Carnot, Prieur (de la Côte-d'Or), and Lindet were replaced by Prieur (de la Marne), Guyton-Morveau, and Richard. Carnot and Lindet, though no longer on the Committee, continued their responsibilities with the personnel, direction, and provisioning of the armies.

New political groupings gradually developed in the Convention after July 27. The Thermidorians of the extreme left, such as Barère, Billaud-Varenne and Collot d'Herbois, wanted to preserve the dictatorship of the Great Committee, continue the Terror, keep the restrictions on private wealth, and maintain the economic controls. More moderate Thermidorians, including Merlin (Douai), Barras, Cambacérès, Siéyès, Tallien, and Fréron opposed the terrorists. Their number was increased on December 9 by the return of the seventy-three deputies imprisoned in the previous year for protesting the expulsion of the Girondins. The surviving Girondin deputies were restored to the Convention on March 8, 1795. A few deputies even favored the restoration of the monarchy. "Carnot and Lindet," writes Aulard, "apparently wanted to rise above these quarrels and play the role of arbiters and establish a liberal republic."[38] For Lindet, at least, this was unexceptional.

Lindet was chosen by the Committees of Public Safety, General Security, and Legislation to prepare and give a joint report on the state of the nation. Lindet read this important state paper to the Convention on September 20.[39] It was widely circulated in French, English and Italian. "Citizens, the representatives of the people have felt the necessity of presenting, in the major epochs of the Revolution, the situation in France; they are eager to make known the causes that have prepared or occasioned these great events. This is an accounting we make to the nation; herein we remind ourselves of what we have been and what we are; we declare what we would become. France listens and will judge us . . . The nation that wants to be free must be strong and powerful enough to resist

38. F.-A. Aulard, *Histoire Politique de la Révolution Française, 1789–1804* (Paris: Librairie Armand Colin, 1905), p. 523; cf. William Finley Shepard, *Price Control and the Reign of Terror in France, 1793–1795* (Berkeley: University of California Press, 1953), p. 35.

39. *Moniteur*, XXII, 18–26. The report was also published as pamphlets by the Imprimerie Nationale in French in twenty-six pages, in English in fifty-seven pages, and in Italian. Each member of the Convention was given six copies of the report and copies were sent to the armies, to the municipalities, to the constituted authorities, and to the popular societies. The report was also printed in England as Robert Lindet *Present State of France*, Report of the Committees of Public and General Safety and of Legislation on the State of France: Presented to the National Convention, September 20th, 1794, by Robert Lindet. (London: John Bell, 1794), 33 pages. Price, one shilling.

the coalition of oppressors and tyrants, compelling them to respect its liberty . . . You have done everything for liberty . . . You have won the support of the peoples . . . This sentiment which you have inspired in the peoples of the North, Africa, and America, as well as your neighbors, expresses itself with *éclat* . . .

"By what means has France arrived at this state of glory and power? . . . When liberty and equality were solemnly proclaimed every Frenchman felt he had a *patrie* and wanted to dedicate himself to her. Every citizen became a defender and supporter of his country. You have reminded men that all are equal, all are brothers. They come to the support of each other . . . as a single family. France, closely united, has become the first and most powerful of nations . . .

"What should impress us is the sublime good sense of the people which has imposed on itself the great privations that have made it possible to establish a regulated economy, so severe and burdensome . . . Its courage has never wavered. It has suffered in order to be free. What a picture to give posterity of a people that offered to the *patrie* continuing sacrifices . . . that surpassed human powers!

"You [Convention] encourage the people, sustain its hope . . . You give laws worthy of a free people; you hold in your firm hands the forces of a vast administration; you prepare and direct the movements that attract the attention of all peoples, and which are changing the face of Europe . . . The spirit of Factionalism reappeared and endangered the *patrie*."

Lindet recalled the powerful Girondin faction and summarized the factions to July 27, saying there had "developed in these very walls the cunning plan of a vast conspiracy. They [conspirators] tried to divide the French, create discouragement, terror, and despair, weaken the gratitude due to the defenders of the country, and spread doubts concerning their victories; they took advantage of their great reputations for talent, energy, and *civisme*. The next day the veil was rent . . .

"The day of 9 Thermidor teaches posterity that France had traversed all the periods of its revolution; that it had come to its conclusion where no one could attempt to mislead except by the force of a great reputation, and the appearance of *civisme*, probity and virtue . . . This latest event was useful to liberty, for the national representation was great and strong enough to destroy the traitors, and the wise, lofty and sublime behavior of the people demonstrated that it is impossible to mislead it . . . Liberate all whom the hates, passions and errors of public officials and the madness of those recent conspirators threw into prison . . ."

Lindet then reviewed the military situation on all fronts and in the Vendée, asked for the revival of commerce and industry at Lyons, Marseilles, Nantes, Bordeaux, and Sedan, called attention to the great need of food and supplies and the difficulties in administering restrictions and requisitions with an even hand, requested freedom of exports, seemed to suggest return to freedom in agriculture, commerce, and industry, and stressed the arts and sciences, both for war and peace.

In one passage Lindet reflected that the "errors, mistakes, abuses of power, and arbitrary acts are those not inseparable from great revolutions." He appealed to his fellow deputies: "Dispel the clouds of ignorance, spread enlightenment and education, provide our citizens with the means from which they learn their rights and duties . . . The situation of France reveals a great nation that understands her rights, her interests, the laws of nature and reason, that desires her security and happiness . . . that wishes to establish peace at home, with the respect of neutral and allied nations, and carry terror beyond her frontiers to her enemies."

There is good evidence that Lindet wished to propose the liberation of those accused of federalism, as well as former nobles and priests against whom there were no charges beyond their birth or occupation.[40] He also hoped to prohibit public officers from attending meetings of public societies, and to forbid affiliations of such societies. The Committee, however, declined to accept these proposals on the grounds that the time was not yet ripe.

Lindet concluded the report by proposing eight decrees, most of which called for statements on trade and exports, though one instructed the Committee on Education to prepare a plan for normal schools, to be staffed by the ablest professors, who were to teach

---

40. *Montier, op. cit.*, pp. 256 ff., derived from Lindet's private papers, confirmed by Georges Lefebvre, *Les Thermidoriens* (Paris: Librairie Armand Colin, 1937), pp. 30–31.

all branches of human knowledge to the most enlightened and
promising students. The decrees were adopted "unanimously and
with the greatest applause."

It was a conciliatory, sober and realistic document, given in the
post-9 Thermidor mood of moderation. It was replete with revolutionary principles, maxims, ideals and phrases. Montier terms it
a "capital piece in the history of the revolutionary government . . .
It is a faithful and impartial witness to the mood in which the
Convention found itself on the morrow of 9 Thermidor. The royalist reaction had not yet succeeded in confiscating the Thermidorian
revolution to its advantage . . ." The report was a "veritable
triumph for Lindet . . . The era of hates and reprisals seemed to
be definitely concluded."[41]

The hope expressed above was not fulfilled. Shortly after July
27, attacks on the "Terrorists" of the two great Committees began.
Lecointre, an excitable Thermidorian, proposed the impeachment
of the members on August 29, but the Convention was not yet
ready. He levelled his attack on Billaud-Varenne, Collot d'Herbois,
Barère, Vadier, Amar, Voulland, and David. He renewed his
campaign on October 7, this time including Carnot.

Lindet, sensitive to the accusations made by the Thermidorians,
felt called upon on October 22 in the Convention to explain and
defend his role in the purge of the Girondins on May 31 and
June 2. His defense was interrupted frequently by exceptions and
protests from members friendly to the Girondins.[42]

"The day of May 31 was grand, happy, useful and necessary,"
Lindet said. ". . . For a long time France had demanded a constitution, which our dissensions obstructed the hope of ever achieving . . . The Sections of Paris singled out twenty-two members as
enemies of the people. These members—who enjoyed great influence and talents—believed they should create a terrible tribunal,
the Commission of Twelve, which threatened public liberty . . .
Disorganization prevailed in the Convention, days passed in sterile
debate; it was no longer possible to act or to promote the welfare
of the people, who wanted a constitution. All Paris desired the
arrest of the twenty-two members." Lindet reminded the Conven-

41. Montier, *op. cit.*, pp. 252, 255–6.
42. *Moniteur*, XXII, 307–8.

tion that he had urged it from Lyons, to "enlighten France as to the motives for the arrest of the twenty-two members, for this is a prime cause of division in the departments." After his speech, debate was closed and the Convention passed to the order of the day.

It was apparent, by now that the former members of the two great Committees were to be under continual scrutiny and attack. The next move came on December 24, when the two Committees reported that there were grounds for investigating the suspicions against Billaud-Varenne, Collot d'Herbois, and Barère of the Committee of Public Safety, and Vadier of the Committee of General Security. The Convention responded by appointing a Committee of Twenty-one to conduct the inquiry. The committee brought in its report on March 2, recommending that the four suspects be arrested, and such was decreed.[43]

The Thermidorians turned their attention to the Law of the Maximum in November. By this time the Subsistence Commission had virtually "withered away," but the Committees of Commerce, Legislation, and Public Safety focussed their attention on the Maximum. In their name, on November 4 Lindet proposed a new method of fixing the Maximum to the Convention, based on differences in fertility and productivity of soil rather than on a uniform price for all of France. He proposed the price level of 1790, by departments and districts, augmented by one-half over and above that price. He questioned the continued need for the Maximum but concluded that it was still necessary, to meet human needs, and to prevent the unrestrained avarice, speculation and abuses that would accompany a premature resumption of the free circulation of grains.[44]

No action was taken on the proposal other than having it printed for later debate. Three days later, Lindet, speaking for the Committees of Public Safety, and Finance, re-introduced the proposal. After extended and lively debate, an amendment to increase the price of grain by two-thirds the price of 1790 was adopted. After debates on following days, the modified proposal was approved on

43. *Moniteur*, XXIII, 584, 589–592.
44. *Moniteur*, XXII, 424.

November 9.[45] Those favoring the return to free trade and economic liberalism were not satisfied with this outcome. A month
later, on December 9, Giraud, in the Committee of Commerce,
Agriculture, and the Arts, proposed the suppression of the Maximum. Lindet, though chairman of the Committee, declined to
sign the *procès-verbal*, resigned the chairmanship and left the
committee. Georges Lefebvre comments: "The decisive defeat of
the men of 1794 was underlined by the retirement of Lindet."[46]
Final action came when the Convention, after extended debate,
repealed the Law of the Maximum on December 24.[47]

The effects of the repeal were immediate and grave. The value
of the assignats collapsed, with all the attendant dislocations. There
followed an "unbridled rise in the price of grain, and extravagant
stock-jobbing."[48] Jacques Godechot points out the effects on the
troops in his analysis of desertions during these months: "Why
these desertions? First, because of the misery of the soldier. The
abandonment of economic regulations after 9 Thermidor, made
the feeding of the armies difficult. The soldiers, poorly paid in
assignats, could not supplement their rations. As a result of the
frauds of the contractors, the soldier was more and more poorly
clad."[49] Lefebvre writes that the abandonment of the controlled
economy produced a "frightful catastrophe . . . The Republic
was condemned to massive inflation that ruined the currency . . .
The famine terribly aggravated the crisis."[50] Sydney Seymour Biro
reports that the "winter of 1794–95 was the hardest since 1709,"
and that on January 5 the police reported that the "people were
complaining that the prices in Paris had doubled since the repeal
of the Maximum only eleven days before."[51]

45. *Moniteur*, XXII, 456–8, 469–470.
46. Lefebvre, *Les Thermidoriens, op. cit.*, p. 95.
47. *Moniteur*, XXIII, 41–48.
48. Montier, *op. cit.*, p. 261.
49. Jacques Godechot, *La Grande Nation—L'Expansion Révolutionnaire de la France dans le Monde, 1789–1799* (Paris: Aubier, 1956), 2 vols., I, p. 142.
50. Lefebvre, *La Révolution Française*, Peuples et Civilisations. Histoire Générale (Louis Halphen, Philippe Sagnac, André Aymard) (Paris: Presses Universitaires de France, 1963), 3ème Éd., pp. 439–440.
51. Sydney Seymour Biro, *The German Policy of Revolutionary France*: A Study in French Diplomacy during the War of the First Coalition, 1792–1797 (Cambridge: Harvard University Press, 1957), 2 vols., I, pp. 259,

In the late winter and early spring of 1795, the Thermidorians returned to their attacks upon the former members of the two great Committees. Billaud-Varenne, Collot d'Herbois, Barère, and Vadier—arrested on March 2—were brought to trial in the Convention on March 22, The question was whether they were to be held equally accountable with Robespierre, Saint-Just, and Couthon for what the Thermidorians thought were the excesses and abuses of the Terror. The galleries were full and the spectators, particularly the "Gilded Youth," sang lustily the new song, *le Réveil du Peuple*, and the *hymne des Marseillais*. The president opened the session to great applause and to shouts of *Vive la Convention! Vive la République!*[52] Outside the hall the *sans-culottes* were clamouring for bread and the Constitution of 1793.

Lindet took the floor on behalf of his accused colleagues, saying in a prepared speech: "Inasmuch as you would judge the government, you should judge it in its integrity; I was a member from the beginning up to October 6 [1794] and although I have been excluded from the accusation of the prisoners, I share their responsibility since I shared their activities." The address took from 12:30 to 6 in the afternoon. Robert Lindet spoke for a couple of hours in his weak voice until he got so tired no one could hear him. His brother Thomas took over and finished reading the manuscript. There were numerous interruptions, both from those who heckled and those who encouraged him. Among the former, Isnard called out "the nation will judge you; you did everything you could to assassinate the *patrie*." Hardy accused Lindet of having "instigated the carnage of Robespierre; it is he who insti-

---

261. Further, for the repeal of the Maximum and the collapse of the assignats see: Bertrand, *La Taxation des Prix, op. cit.*, p. 203; Daniel Guerin, *La Lutte des Classes Sous la Première République*, Bourgeois et "bras nus" (1793–1797) (Paris: Gallimard, 1946), 2 vols., II, p. 314. Guerin recognizes Lindet's abilities but is unfavorable to him, considering him a deceiver of the masses as "protector of the men of affairs." Albert Mathiez, *La Réaction Thermidorrienne* (Paris: Librairie Armand Colin, 1929), pp. 187–196; Marcel Marion, *Histoire Financière de la France depuis 1715*. Tome III, 1792–1797. (Paris: Rousseau et Cie., 2me éd.); Käre D. Tonnesson, *La Défaite des Sans-Culottes*: mouvement populaire et réaction bourgeoise en l' an III (Paris: Librairie R. Chauvreuil, 1959), for an excellent detailed account, with an inclusive bibliography.

52. *Moniteur*, XXIV, 43–48.

tuted the revolutionary tribunal." Henri Larivière even shouted "there was no more unbridled royalist than he during the Legislative Assembly."

Lindet pointed out the situation in France at the time the two great Committees were created: "Dumouriez, rebel and traitor, the Vendée in flames, Mont-Blanc invaded, the departments disturbed by baneful dissensions, an army in each district, no longer citizens and brothers, but implacable enemies everywhere." He went into great detail in describing the structure and work of the Committee of Public Safety, outlining the program for provisioning and feeding the armies and France—his own special responsibility—attributing the success of the program to the system of requisitions, and the response of the people to the Law of the Maximum. "I wanted to save Lyons for the republic; I pacified Calvados; I exorcised federalism; I arrested those who wanted to march on Paris: *this* is sufficient for me to die! . . . I declare to you that . . . it is the government as a whole that you should judge . . . Never has anyone extorted from me a shameful disavowal, a retraction which was not in my heart. My writings, my speeches, my actions, I submit to scrutiny; one will find the same constancy of principles, the same steadfastness to defend the liberty of my country; one will find that I have never counselled violent or sanguinary measures; such are not in my character, nor in my thoughts. I had no relations with Robespierre, Couthon and Saint-Just; for a long time I knew how to judge them, and more than one-hundred members of this assembly can attest to my judgment of them. I conclude in recommending a general and detailed report of the conduct of the former government; your security demands it, the wish of the people makes it your duty."

Henri Carré evaluates the address: "The sincerity and courage of [Lindet's] attitude produced a sensation so lively that the assembly voted the printing of the speech, in spite of violent murmurs of the Thermidorians."[53]

Carnot likewise announced the next day that he wanted to stand with his accused associates and share their fate. In his lengthy address he said: "For a long time I personally attacked Robespierre and Saint-Just in the meetings of the Committee of Public

53. Henri Carré, *Le Grand Carnot, op. cit.,* p. 227.

Safety."[54] Carnot and Lindet undoubtedly knew their time would come before the bar of the Convention.

The "insurrection" of the *sans-culottes* on April 1, and the invasion of the assembly hall by a multitude of women and unarmed men, denouncing hoarders and profiteers, and demanding bread and the Constitution of 1793, so alarmed the Convention that, when the National Guard had restored order by nightfall, it declared Billaud-Varenne, Collot d'Herbois, Barère, and Vadier guilty and condemned them to deportation, without a vote and by acclamation. Barère escaped and the others were sent to Guiana.

The attack on the remaining members of the former Committees was renewed in late May. In a tumultuous session of the Convention on May 20, the galleries were full of women crying: "Bread, we want bread;" several arrests were made. Hardy rose to make a bold accusation: "There still exists a monster in our midst—it is Robert Lindet. I do not believe there is a greater enemy of liberty . . . He is the craftiest of men. I demand his arrest."[55] Thomas Lindet came to the defense of his brother: "My brother has been denounced but he has done nothing nor said anything. Today, let us review his missions and his activities in the Committee of Public Safety; *eh bien*, let us consult the departments of the Eure and Calvados, and the city of Lyons . . . and I am convinced that no one will accuse him of committing any action which has harmed humanity." On the motion of Pierret, the Convention passed to the order of the day.

Henri Larivière entered the lists the next day, accusing Robert Lindet of being involved in organizing the public clamor in the hall on the previous day. In his reply Lindet declared: "I have never been a member of any society."[56] Hardy again attacked on May 28, denouncing Lindet and Jean-Bon Saint-André as among the conspirators responsible for the disorders of April and May. Gamon spoke of the "presence of assassins of the *patrie* in the very bosom of the Convention." Larivière followed in a general condemnation of the former members of the Great Committee, holding them all responsible for the excesses of the Terror, admit-

54. *Moniteur*, XXIV, 47–53.
55. *Moniteur*, XXIV, 514.
56. *Ibid.*, 520.

ting, however, that there were three groups in the Committee, one of which was composed of Carnot, Lindet, and Prieur (de la Côte-d'Or). He specifically challenged Carnot: "How could you be so indifferent, or so imbecile, as not to open your eyes to the projects of the cannibals with whom you were associated? Not to prevent crime is to commit it." Carnot in his reply repeated what he had claimed earlier: "I was confined constantly to the task for which I was responsible; I worked sixteen hours a day, and I had no ear for anything but what happened in my offices; . . . As for signatures, I gave them as of confidence, and that is still being done today; it was impossible to examine the papers that were presented to me to sign."

Gouly, after a lengthy preamble, called for the arrest of Lindet, Voulland, Saint-André, Jagot, Elie Lacoste, Lavicomterie, David, Carnot, Prieur, Barbau-Dubarran, and Bernard—de Saintes—all members of the two Committees. Prieur (de la Côte-d'Or) spoke for the first time: "General measures always include the innocent. I have not hitherto asked to share the fate of the former members . . . but just imagine what a great day for the royalists this will be, if . . ." Violent murmurs stifled the conclusion of the sentence.

In the turbulence, Taveau and Doulcet of Calvados, came to the defense of Lindet by reminding the assembly of his success in pacifying the Eure and Calvados. Doulcet cautioned his associates: "We should not judge opinions but facts . . . Up to the present we have only struck down our colleagues for positive acts, and there are none against these members of the former government." Larivière replied by calling Lindet the "greatest hypocrite of all." Hardy, although admitting that Lindet had saved his family— declared *hors la loi*—said: "I see only my country and am obliged to pronounce on the crimes which the deputy Lindet has committed against it." In the debate, Lindet affirmed: "I was never the friend of Robespierre; I remained isolated." But when he attempted to speak of his efforts of reconciliation at Lyons, he was shouted down. Dubois-Crancé even accused him of having lost Lyons. The arrest of Robert Lindet was unanimously voted. When the vote on Carnot was called an anonymous voice cried out: "Carnot organized the victory," and the Convention, shamed by the cry, refused to press the matter to a vote. Lindet joined DuRoy in prison, where he prepared his defense.[57]

The fortunes of war, in the meantime, had smiled on French arms. Prussia sued for peace late in 1794, and negotiations were concluded on April 5 with the Treaty of Basle. The Dutch agreed to French terms on May 16 in the Treaty of the Hague.

Pending the disposition of his case Lindet was granted provisional liberty from prison because of a severe intestinal ailment, probably aggravated by "cruel mental anguish."[58] During this period, friends and others, recipients of his services, interceded on his behalf in the Convention. The Commune of Evreux memorialized the assembly, denying that Lindet was a terrorist, and affirming that he had saved those sent to the Revolutionary Tribunal from Evreux and Conches.[59] The Commune of Conches sent an address to the Convention, declaring: "He was our defender, our protection, and we pay but a feeble tribute for the gratitude we owe him."[60] Citizens of Caen petitioned the Convention, and merchants from Nantes appeared before the assembly to support his loyalty to the Revolution.

Merchants of Havre memorialized the Convention on August 13, urging the release of Lindet, in consideration of services he had rendered that city. In the disorderly session, Hardy questioned the signatures and accused Lindet of having secretly distributed grain in Havre and Rouen, to make friends, should affairs go against the conspirators. He called Lindet the "most guilty of the Decemvirs. It was he who purged our colleagues." The Girondin Delahaye called Lindet "more sly, but no less nefarious, than the others." It was alleged in the session that Thomas Lindet had solicited the signatures of the merchants. He replied on the floor: "Never in my life have I spoken to the petitioners . . . It is astonishing that when all France acclaims Robert Lindet . . ." Protests prevented him from continuing. Hardy called the petitioners "intriguers." Charge and counter-charge flew back and forth

57. *Moniteur*, XXIV, 570–574, for this turbulent session.
58. M. L. Boivin-Champeaux, *Les Fédéralistes, op. cit.*, p. 27
59. Rogne, *Souvenirs, op. cit.*, p. 101.
60. Montier, *op. cit.*, p. 290.

until the report concludes: "The Convention continued for some time in tumult and agitation" until the assembly passed to the order of the day.[61]

Lindet had two versions of his defense published, one in June on order of the Convention, and the other at his own expense.[62] In the latter he stated the charges against him and proceeded to answer them, one by one. Among the charges were: provoking violence and maintaining a directory of conspiracy in Caen, presiding over an assembly of conspirators in April and May, 1795, responsibility for the ruin of Lyons, initiator of the revolutionary tribunal without a jury, organizer of the famine in France, and being a barbarian thirsting for 200,000 heads.

Lindet's defense was a sober array of facts and rebuttal in which he attempted to disassociate himself from the triumvirs, considering them the lesser of the evils in his efforts to fulfill the tasks assigned to him for the good of France. To the accusation of participating in various conspiracies, he replied: "It is known that I belong to no society, that I never attended the Cordeliers or the Jacobins; it is known that I formed no group in the Convention or outside it; I did not attend spectacles, nor promenades, nor the faubourgs of Paris. It is said that I was the author of the ruin of Lyons . . . There is no one of you who can ignore that I alone had the courage to reveal the cause of the troubles in Lyons; that I alone advised that the way of reconciliation would lead to order and tranquillity, that all hostility was a crime . . .

"I did everything it was possible to do . . . to supply and maintain 1,200,000 men under arms, and a million men employed in the services and arts of war; supply and feed the communes, repair the damages occasioned by the invasion of the Prussians and Austrians . . . and by the irruption in the Vendée . . . There was nothing in common between myself and the other members of the government . . . I was never the associate of those who exercised the tyranny, but stayed in the dangerous post confided to me, only to save France . . . My conduct was always pure and constant . . ."

---

61. *Moniteur*, XXV, 502–3.

62. R. Lindet, répresentant du peuple, à la Convention Nationale, S. L. 1795; also extensively quoted in Montier, *op. cit.*, pp. 295–304. The official version ran to fourteen pages, the other to thirty.

"A representative of the people," he concluded, "is only accountable to his conscience for his opinions. He fulfills his duty when, in the clash of opinions and events, and compelled to act, he knows how to judge what is possible and not possible, and, beset by the gloom which presses upon him in his isolation, he never loses sight of the spirit of preservation, and applies himself to save all when there is danger of losing all. Representatives, you will not wish to violate in my case the principle you have consecrated for yourselves and for all of France."

In a supplementary defense, speaking of himself in the third person, Lindet wrote: "The National Convention rendered justice to Carnot, for he organized victory, but he did not organize it alone; R. Lindet provided the food, equipment, clothing, waggons, and transports without which what would have become of our armies?" He defended himself against the odium of requisitions and the Maximum by saying the Maximum had been decreed in his absence, he had to work with the means legally given him, and he had done the best he could under the circumstances, to give freedom to cultivators and merchants.[63]

Lindet was liberated by the amnesty of October 24. He published a pamphlet—"Essay on the Public Credit and Subsistence" —at the time, in which he blamed the government for the planned depreciation of the assignats that "ruined the country."[64] Somewhat later, he issued a forty-three page pamphlet, "Robert Lindet— au peuple français ou Tableau de la Convention nationale," an ardent and eloquent exposition of his conduct during the Convention. "I served the *patrie* without glory, without repute, but without stain and without reproach . . . I was associated neither with the fame nor the crimes of any of my colleagues." He repeated earlier defenses against the accusations levelled against him in May, giving particular attention to those that associated him with the establishment of the Revolutionary Tribunal. He spoke of the war declared on England as "unjustly undertaken, but which had to be supported."[65]

Lindet left the Convention, according to Montier, poorer than

63. Montier, *op. cit.*, pp. 304–6.
64. *Ibid.*, pp. 310–311.
65. Paris: Quatrième année de l'Ère Républicaine.

he had been in 1791. On October 13, 1795, he made a declaration of his fortune, in conformity to the decree of September 25. His personal property in 1791, when he was elected to the Legislative Assembly, totalled 43,000 livres, of which there barely remained 22,000 in 1795. More than half the 22,000 was in the hands of debtors without interest and with little hope of repayment. His small farms at Plasnes alone remained intact. He had not been reimbursed for the 1,200 francs he had advanced for his expenses when on mission to the Eure and Calvados in the summer of 1793, nor for the 1,350 francs which he had paid for the printing of the two pamphlets in his defense in the summer of 1795.[66]

Ten days after making this financial statement and two weeks before the dissolution of the Convention, Lindet posted in the halls of the Convention his "Compte Rendu par R. Lindet, de son mandat de député à la Convention." "There were few representatives," he declared, "who contributed as much as I to support the war against the coalition, in a manner useful and glorious for France, although I did not approve the war so unjustly declared on England . . . I never promoted the civil war; I was not among those who wished to support their opinions by force of arms . . . I have never been a theologian, academician, philosopher, or orator, but I have declared that it was not permissible to teach or support atheism publicly. Politics has seemed to me to be a vast open field for all thinking persons . . . The best religion, the most sublime politics, consists to me, in courage of mind, in good judgment, and in irreproachable conduct . . . I have not enriched myself, nor any other person; but I have served the Republic which preserves all the goods, all the fortunes, and guarantees to all citizens of all classes the means of subsistence, and to the legitimate creditors of the state the reimbursement of their loans and advances."[67]

The *compte rendu* was a combination of continued defense against his political enemies, philosophical reflections, and some self-praise. Thus the sincere and sober Republican brought to a

66. A. Mathiez, "La Fortune de Robert Lindet," *Annales Révolutionnaires*, XII, 1920, pp. 66–67, for a detailed treatment of this financial declaration; Albert Mathiez, *La Réaction Thermidorienne* (Paris: Librairie Armand Colin, 1929), pp. 266 ff; Montier, *op cit.*, pp. 314–315.

67. Montier, *op. cit.*, pp. 316–320, from the papers of Robert Lindet.

conclusion his practical and useful career in the climactic and decisive years of the national Convention. Robert Lindet had been an inconspicuous but important member of the Committee of Public Safety during the Terror, when the Committee had exercised a genuine dictatorship over a subservient Convention and over a submissive France. As a war cabinet it had mobilized and utilized the total resources of the country for the consolidation of the Revolution and for the defense of the *patrie*. Under the dictatorship the democratic First Republic had been established, the Revolution had been saved, France had been defended against the multiple Powers of the Coalition, the civil war had been checked, and the regeneration of France, and the Republic of Virtue had been planned. The "nation in arms," too, had given birth to that new phenomenon, French popular nationalism, the harbinger of nationalism in Europe in the next century. Despite these great services, rendered in the heat of Revolution after the destruction of the monarchy, the dictatorship of the Great Committee left a France divided and much unfinished business for the turbulent years ahead.

CHAPTER SIX

Republicans to the End, 1795 - 1825

ROBERT LINDET'S PUBLIC CAREER did not end completely with the inauguration of the Directory. He was asked by the new government to accept confidential and administrative posts but declined. Persecution by his political enemies continued, compelling him to defend himself. He was accused of being implicated in the "Babeuf Plot," was tried *in absentia* before the High Court, and was acquitted. Finally, he was appointed Minister of Finance shortly before Bonaparte's *coup d'état* of 18 Brumaire—November 8, 1799. But the staunch republican abhorred this betrayal of the Revolution and refused to have anything to do with Napoleonic dictatorship in any of its forms.

Throughout the vicissitudes of the incompetent and corrupt Directory, and the anti-republican regimes of the Consulate, Empire, and Bourbon Restoration—with a seeming lapse under the last-named—Lindet remained true to his character of moderate and faithful republican until his death in 1825 at seventy-nine. He had paid the price for his convictions and he persevered in them to the end. He was happy to return to private life but grieved at the reverses the hard-won revolutionary principles and institutions suffered in the last thirty years of his life.

Lindet was elected to the Legislative Corps on October 15, 1795, by the Department of the Nord, as well as by the Section of the Oratoire in Paris, but the Thermidorians declared these elections void since he was ineligible under the terms of the amnesty. Thomas, on the other hand, was elected on October 13 to the Council of Elders by the Department of the Eure, and served for two years, when the Directory named him its executive Commissioner in the Eure. The five Directors asked Robert, on the invitation of Carnot on November 6, to serve as secret agent in Basle. Lindet refused, saying that if it was to spy, the answer was "no," and if it was a means to exile him, the answer was also "no." Carnot then offered him, on November 23, the post of Commissioner of the Directory in the Eure.[1]

The Directory administered France through local commissioners whom it appointed, often selecting them on recommendations from the departments. Robert Lindet's name was on the first list of nominations, but he refused to accept the appointment.[2] Carnot wrote on December 1, urging him to accept: "Your wish to return to your region accords with that of the Directory and of your compatriots . . . I invoke my esteem and attachment for you; I limit myself to saying that you are needed." Lindet still declined: "I refused this offer for I did not want to assume responsibility for bankruptcy or famine . . . I could not accept since it was only a matter of consummating misfortune. I wanted to know what course the Legislative Corps was going to take with reference to the assignats. That would be decisive. I did not cease my efforts to prevent bankruptcy and oppose the measures of the swindlers." Montier reports that Carnot seemed to be much offended by this refusal and never forgave Lindet, the proof coming, avers Montier, in the Babeuf affair.[3]

The "men of 1794," including the Subsistence Commission, were attacked by Eschessériaux on November 13 in the Council of Five Hundred in a speech on the state of the finances. Lindet defended the Commission in a long letter from Paris: "You charge the Commission and those responsible for its surveillance and direction with capital crimes . . . You reproach the Commission for causing the destruction of the economy through false principles. The Commission was obliged to conform to your laws . . . All precautions were taken to prevent abuses . . . The Commission was created because everything was lacking; it was impossible to pro-

---

1. Montier, *op. cit.*, p. 322.
2. Aulard, *Histoire Politique, op. cit.*, p. 605.
3. Montier, *op. cit.*, pp. 322, 325.

vision Paris; the armies were completely destitute; our territory was invaded; the civil war in the west, the siege of Lyons, and the capture of Toulon all caused a prodigious consumption and an extreme scarcity in most of France . . . What an injustice to say today that it is the Commission that was responsible for these deficiencies . . ."

Lindet assumed full responsibility for the direction of the Commission from November 7, 1793, to the end of September, 1795. He claimed that the fall of the assignats, the decline of the economy, and the corruption and cupidity of the gamblers and profiteers developed after the suppression of the Commission and his departure from the government. He concluded by demanding that he be brought promptly to judgment for his administration; then it would become "known whether it was when I directed subsistence and provisioning that thousands of citizens amassed scandalous fortunes on the ruins of the nation, or whether this happened after my retirement . . ."

Eschassériaux replied, absolving himself from any intention of criticizing Lindet. The latter responded on November 27, again asking that he be judged. Boissy d'Anglas attacked Lindet and the Commission in the *Amis des Lois* on December 1 and 4. Lindet replied in the same journal and had several articles in it criticizing the financial program of the Directory. That on December 25 on the necessity of reducing government expenses, reforming abuses, and eliminating waste, was "full of good sense," avers Montier. Lindet opposed proposals for a bank, not so much in principle as for the type of organization advocated. Dupont de Nemours, furious over this criticism and the failure to establish the bank, violently attacked Lindet in the *Historien* of March 26, 1796, for his role in the Committee of Public Safety, and Lindet replied in the *Amis des Lois*.[4]

Lindet was subjected to a new attack in the spring of 1796. The complicated Babeuf affair reached its climax in May. François-Noël "Gracchus" Babeuf, born in 1760 in Picardy, was steeped in Rousseau's works, Morelly's *Code de la Nature*, and the Abbé Mably's *De la Législation*. These studies and his diverse experiences prepared him for the radical, though brief, role he was to play

4. Montier, *op. cit.*, pp. 320–335.

in the Revolution. He was the precursor of modern socialism, both Utopian and "scientific." David Thomson writes that through his whole life ran a "constant thread of passionate sincerity and integrity of purpose."[5]

As early as 1787 Babeuf gave evidence of egalitarian, communalist ideas. He was active in the preparation of the *Cahier* for Roye in 1789. He did some pamphleteering early in the Revolution. In 1794, he came to Paris from Amiens, as secretary in the Bureau of Subsistence of the Paris Commune. After 9 Thermidor he launched his *Journal de la Liberté de la Presse*, in which he attacked Robespierre and the Commune. His paper came under suspicion and on September 3, 1794, he changed its name to *Tribune du Peuple, ou Le Défenseur des Droits de l'Homme*. He went into hiding but the police found and seized him on February 15, 1795. Imprisoned at first in Arras, he was transferred to Paris in September, where he was released under the amnesty of the Convention at its last session.

The Society of the Panthéon became mixed up in the Babeuf affair. This society was formed in the fall of 1795, meeting in the crypt of the Convent of Sainte-Geneviève, and including two groups: the left wing of followers of Babeuf, interested in achieving social and economic equality as well as political; the right wing of disgruntled former Jacobins who opposed the government of the Directory, sought revenge against the reactionary forces of Thermidor, and favored the democratic Constitution of 1793. Babeuf's actual association with the Society is uncertain. The members read his *Tribune du Peuple*, and the *Amis des Lois* was friendly to them.

Babeuf, his journal, and the Society became the objects of police action early in 1796. The Directory dissolved the Society, the *Tribune du Peuple* ceased publication, and Babeuf evaded arrest. In late March he founded the Insurrectionary Committee with five

5. David Thomson, *The Babeuf Plot: The Making of a Republican Legend* (London: Kegan Paul, Trench, Trubner & Co., Ltd., 1947), p. 18. In addition to this excellent volume, the treatment of Babeuf is derived particularly from the following: Gerard Walter, *Babeuf, 1760–1797 et la Conjuration des Égaux* (Paris: Payot, 1937), a fine narrative, objective and balanced, with justice to Babeuf's ideas, and with Babeuf put in a human and humane light; Montier, *Robert Lindet, op. cit.*

other persons, including the Italian Buonarroti. The Committee's *Manifeste des Égaux—Manifesto of Equals*—appeared in April, followed soon by a more incisive and stirring statement of doctrines, attributed to Babeuf. The Manifesto claimed that the French had lived in misery as slaves for fifteen centuries, followed by six years of revolution, the "forerunner of another revolution—far greater, far more solemn, which will be the last."

Then came the heart of the program: "No more individual ownership of land; the land belongs to nobody. We lay claim to, we demand, common enjoyment of the fruits of the earth; the fruits exist for all . . . The moment has come to found the Republic of Equals, that great hospice open to all men . . . Come all ye in distress and be seated at the common table set by nature for all her children . . . The aristocratic charters of 1791 and 1795 rivet your chains instead of breaking them. That of 1793 made a real stride towards true equality."

The Insurrectionary Committee began planning a *coup d'état* but government agents, one of whom was the spy Grisel, discovered the plot. The Directory took speedy action against the Committee and its allies, arresting the Committee members on May 10, and seizing documentary evidence of the plot. Carnot announced the conspiracy to the Council of Five Hundred on the day of the arrests, presenting a list of 245 suspects, of whom 64 were alleged to be involved in the plot. One of the latter was Robert Lindet. The government was successful in arresting only 47 of the 64. The seventeen escaping included Lindet.

The 47 imprisoned "conspirators" were transferred to the Vendôme prison on August 27, where they languished until February 20, 1797, when their trial began, lasting until May 27. The accused were tried by the court and a jury of sixteen. The public soon lost interest and only Babouvist sympathizers attended. The accused freely admitted their beliefs in lengthy speeches, though they denied an actual conspiracy. They ended each day's session by singing republican songs. Babeuf's own defense took four days and covered 300 pages. He and one other were condemned to death, seven were deported, and the others were acquitted. Babeuf's clumsy efforts to stab himself failed and he was guillotined.

Robert Lindet was on the list of those to be arrested in May in

connection with the Babeuf plot. It appears that Lindet had been
meeting with a group that was exploring ways by which the democratic Constitution of 1793 might be substituted for that of 1795,
as the only means of fulfilling the Revolution of 1789. A connection was alleged between this group and the Babeuf conspirators.
Soboul believes there was more to it than this: "The 'Conspiracy
of the Equals,' grouped around Babeuf all the dissidents of the
left, former *Enragés* like Sylvain Maréchal, former Montagnards
such as Lindet, Amar, Drouet . . . former Robespierrists such as
Buonarroti . . . This opposition took on a revolutionary tone."[6]
Gerard Walter involves Lindet in a meeting of about fifteen persons, members of the "Directoire secret," on May 8 at which, he
says, Babeuf demanded a date for the insurrection. "One of the
ex-conventionnels present, Robert Lindet, dwelt at length on the
necessity of remembering their proscribed and guillotined colleagues." Walter indicates that this and other speeches revealed
that some of those present were not "strictly informed of the
revolutionary activity being unfolded by the Directoire secret."
He classifies the twenty-four active leaders of the "conspiracy"
into four groups, and the "sympathizers" into two—active and
passive. Since he did not list Lindet among the active leaders or
the active sympathizers he apparently included him in the passive
group.[7] Grisel's evidence on the plotters, at least on Lindet, was
proven to be suspect in the trial of Lindet *in absentia*. David
Thomson does not mention Lindet as one of those actually involved in the Babeuf plot.

It seems reasonable to conclude on the evidence of his private
and public life, that support by Lindet of the radical social program of Babeuf and of a *coup d'état* to usher in a communalist
regime would have been utterly alien to his background and convictions and quite out of character with his temperament.

Lindet evaded arrest and fled Paris. He was given asylum in
the home of Pierre Mesnil in Caen. Mesnil had been an administrator of the Department of Calvados who was compromised in
the old federalist movement. At that time Lindet had saved him

6. Albert Soboul, *La Révolution Française, 1789–1799* (Paris: Editions
Sociales, 1948), p. 318.
7. Walter, *op. cit.*, pp. 144, 157, 256.

from the Revolutionary Tribunal. Mesnil was a bourgeois who was sympathetic to the common people. When it was safe to do so, Mesnil wrote a warm letter to Lindet's sister: "We have the precious privilege of enjoying for some time a friend whose virtues have been the cause of persecutions . . . His courage, his humanity, his talents, his delicacy are the very things that have aroused the serpents of envy against him. In 1793 he saved our departments from the imminent danger that threatened them, and I share with my colleagues the fruit of his solicitude. He saved us, Madame, and no administrator perished. You surmise that I speak of M. Lindet, your brother. We beg you to come visit him."[8]

Lindet was tried *in absentia* before the High Court, with the others accused. He was acquitted on May 25 for lack of evidence. His only denunciator was the agent, Grisel. Thomas Lindet, in in defense of his brother, exposed Grisel's testimony as false, attributing the inclusion of Lindet in the group to political vengeance. Aulard states that "Grisel denounced Robert Lindet [at the trial] as having attended the meeting of May 8 but, cross-examined concerning the description of Lindet, Grisel said that he had white hair, when he had black hair."[9]

Thomas Lindet addressed two memoirs to the High Court of Justice on behalf of his brother.[10] The first was largely a warm, general defense of Robert's public career: "I have fulfilled a sacred duty. I have undertaken the justification of one who is dear to me and who should be dear to all friends of the *patrie.*" In the second documents, Thomas gave more attention to the current accusations, after having explained Robert's absence from the trial because of poor health. In part, Thomas said: "Robert Lindet neither knew nor had ever seen Grisel; he knew neither Babeuf or Massard, nor most of the accused; he had never had any relations with them and had visited none of them. He saw Choudieu only once

8. Montier, *op. cit.*, p. 355.
9. Aulard, *Histoire Politique, op. cit.*, p. 633; Georges Bouchard, *Prieur de la Côte-D'Or* (Paris: Librairie Historique R. Clavreuil, 1946), p. 449, also attests to Robert Lindet's innocence in this affair.
10. Robert-Thomas Lindet-Représentant du Peuple, à la Haute-Court de Justice, sur l'accusation contre Robert Lindet (Paris: De l'Imprimerie de la rue Honoré, No. 2, s.d.), 28 pages; Robert-Thomas Lindet, Second Mémoire pour Robert Lindet, accusé devant la Haute-Court de Justice (Evreux: Imprimerie de Touquet, s.d.), 10 pages.

in the Committee of Public Safety, where he [Lindet] had opposed his views on the war in the Vendée, and had never spoken to him since . . . R. Lindet dwelt in a house adjacent to that of Drouet; he had never entered the latter . . ." Thomas reported that Robert's enemies sought revenge, mentioning Henri Larivière specifically in this connection.

When the case was concluded, Thomas wrote to his brother: "The High Court has acquitted you, you are finally free . . . But you have cruel and powerful enemies, inaccessible to remorse and shame . . . Lemercier said, during the course of the trial: 'We have pardoned R. Lindet a second time; the third time he will die.' Receive the tender and sincere embrace of my wife."[11]

Robert Lindet was "touched by the grace and beauty" of Marie-Agathe-Elizabeth Mesnil during the time he had asylum in the Mesnil home in Caen, and he came to love her. He was fifty-three at the time and she was nearly twenty years younger. The suitor hesitated to pursue the matter because of his precarious financial state. But in early April, 1798, he was elected to the Council of the Five Hundred from the Eure, through the campaigning of his brother, while the latter was elected to the Council of Elders. Robert was also exploring the possibility of a government post through Merlin (de Douai), one of the Directors. With the parliamentary assurance and the hope of an official appointment, Lindet secured the consent of the daughter's sympathetic parents to press his suit, which he did in a warm and eloquent letter of proposal on April 19: "Mademoiselle, my happiness begins. Your mother and father know and have the kindness to approve my feelings. Your heart, your hand are the unique gift to which I aspire; your acquiescence will make me happy. Permit me, I pray, to tell you what chagrin, what anxiety consumes me [he goes on to bewail his scant material resources] . . . Only your welfare concerns me. I have all my life been too indifferent, too unconcerned, about myself; here is the source of the grief and the sorrow that has troubled me since I have been in your home. My most tender inclination each day has been to aspire to responsibility for your happiness. What a task for me! . . . You, alone, fill my thoughts, and fear is destroying me . . . You will find that the pledge of my

11. Montier, *op. cit.*, pp. 354–5.

promises, my engagements to you are sacred. Your happiness will be mine: I will not be, I cannot be, happy excepting when the smile on your lips tells me of your satisfaction. I live, I breathe for you . . . Your inseparable friend. R. Lindet."[12]

Elizabeth accepted his offer and they were married in the *Mairie* of Caen on May 7, 1798. Three days later the Legislative Corps annulled the election of the two brothers because of some alleged irregularity in Robert's search for a government post. The couple had hoped to settle in Evreux or on his farm at Plasnes, near Bernay. Thomas wrote to dissuade him: "You will not find security here. Evreux has been the seat of a great intrigue against you. At present, we could become traduced . . . The fire has not been extinguished. You should not risk it." The newly-married couple then established themselves in simple quarters in Paris where Robert took up a modest practice as a consulting lawyer. Arsenne, a much-beloved daughter, was born on April 16, 1799.[13]

Thomas Lindet, former priest, bishop, and legislator, studied law in Paris during the early years of the Directory, thereafter returning to Bernay to practice his new profession. Upon the death of his adored daughter he gave up the law, living in retirement on his modest patrimony and certain life annuities.

Robert Lindet was called back into public service briefly when the Directory nominated him to be Minister of Finance on July 23, 1799. Two days later he accepted and on July 29 took the oath of office.[14] This choice was applauded in the Paris papers. The finances of the government were in a very sad state. "The treasury was empty," reports Montier; "It was necessary to take urgent measures to procure funds."[15]

The Directory convoked a meeting of most of the leading bank-

---

12. Montier, *op. cit.*, p. 357. The letter is in the Bibliothèque of Caen.
13. *Ibid.*, pp. 358–360.
14. *Moniteur*, XXIX, 747, 755. Thomas wrote his brother from Bernay, trying to dissuade him from taking the post, saying that if he succeeded in restoring the finances he would be more skilful than Sully because there were more obstacles to overcome. He wrote an affectionate letter to Robert's wife for the same purpose, appealing to her because of the "reign which you have over his heart." Montier, *op. cit.*, pp. 367–368. For the appointment also see Marcel Marion, *Histoire Financière de la France depuis 1715* (Paris: Rousseau et Cie., 1927), Tome IV, 1797–1818, 2me. éd., p. 150.
15. Montier, *op. cit.*, p. 370.

ers on July 30 to discuss the financial crisis, but nothing was decided at the session. They re-assembled the next evening with the new Minister of Finance. The meeting lasted until midnight, adjourning after having named commissioners to study the request for thirty millions from the bankers. These commissioners agreed to form a syndicate and put thirty millions of bonds and notes at the disposition of the Directory.[16]

The situation Lindet faced in the Ministry was vividly described in the *Journal des Hommes Libres* on August 4: ". . . There was no administration in which royalism had as many partisans as in the Ministry of Finance. Most of the bureau heads were the same as under Calonne and Necker; the others were the choice of Amelot [appointed by the King on April 25, 1790]; when he organized the *caisse de l'extraordinaire*, he employed a band of lawyers, priests, and swindlers; émigrés, relatives of émigrés, intriguers, thieves, finally, all who were enemies of the Republic . . . They regarded their positions as their patrimony, and it appeared that the Republic paid them to destroy it. It was left to Lindet to introduce the republican spirit into this den where it had never penetrated, and to bring these men into accord with their conscience . . . Let him not be afraid of the cries of the aristocracy against him if he smites the royalist serpent; this he can expect. It will truly be in disestablishing the plans of the thieves and the protectors of the émigrés, that he will create a republican ministry."[17]

The *Amis des Lois* commented on the conduct of Lindet as Minister in its issues of August 6: ". . . The Vatar committee solicits, menaces and intrigues to overthrow the Ministry of Finance, as it has done with those of the interior, of war, and of police; but Robert Lindet, who did not want to be minister, commits no baseness in order to preserve his position. He is master of his ministry, and no Director, nor Jacobin can make him do what he does not judge to be proper in the public interest. His firm, inflexible and just conduct has inspired the greatest confi-

16. A. Aulard, *Paris Pendant la Réaction Thermidorienne et sous le Directoire. Receuil de Documents pour l'Histoire de l'Esprit Public à Paris.* (Paris: Librairie Léopold Cerf, 1902), Tome V, 661–2; Montier, *op. cit.,* p. 370.

17. Aulard, *Paris Pendant, op. cit.,* V, 668.

dence in the men of affairs who have decided to make financial advances to the Republic. 'You may deceive me,' he told them, 'but I shall never deceive you.' Ramel [Ramel-Nogaret, Lindet's predecessor as Minister], on the contrary, never went to bed content until he had deceived someone . . ."[18]

Bonaparte's *coup d'état* of 18 Brumaire—November 8—came just as Lindet was getting the finances in order. He had been in office slightly more than three months. As a committed republican he did not accept the coup. He refused to go to Saint-Cloud. It took a letter from Cambacérès, Minister of Justice, to force him to join his associates, in conformity with the decree on the transfer of power. Gaudin replaced Lindet as Minister of Finance at the first meeting of the three consuls. The consuls had approved Lindet's *compte rendu* two days after the *coup d'état*, and he was given his complete and definitive release on December 12.

Lindet wrote to Mesnil two days after the coup: ". . . In Paris one frequents the spectacles; one grumbles; folly, luxury and misery are neighbors without touching each other. There is not the least appearance of turbulence or uneasiness." In another letter to his father-in-law on December 8, he commented on the coup and outlined the plan he had for the finances: ". . . The consular power which exists today has nothing in common with the consuls of Rome. Those consuls were freely elected. They were a properly constituted authority and they could not destroy nor replace the other authorities. It is not known why Siéyès and Buonaparte have taken the name of consuls . . . If Buonaparte wishes to rule, who is there to prevent him? If Buonaparte dies, who will prevent Moreau from having his generals proclaim him in the name of the army? . . ." He wrote steadily of the need to make peace with England, and commented again on December 23 on the consulate: "I no longer know . . what colors one should hoist: it is the same to me that we have a consul, or a protector, or a prince. The name is immaterial, but it is necessary to know this . . . I abjure all politics . . ."[19]

Napoleon later said of Lindet: "At the time of Brumaire, the Ministry of Finance was held by Robert Lindet, who had been

18. *Ibid.*, 670.
19. Montier, *op. cit.*, pp. 376–8, 379, 383.

a member of the Committee of Public Safety in the time of Robespierre. He was an honest man, but without any of the understanding necessary for the administration of finances for a great empire. Under the revolutionary government, however, he had earned a reputation as a great financier; but under that government the real minister of finances was the overseer of the board of the assignats."[20]

After Bonaparte's coup and Lindet's dismissal, the family moved into very modest lodgings in Paris. Robert's only property was his little farm at Plasnes. Mesnil gladly loaned him money until he built up a practice in Paris, Caen and Rouen. He was gradually able to earn a respectable living and Palmer says he made a fortune of 50,000 francs between his fifty-seventh and seventy-third years.[21]

Who and where were the republicans during the rule of Napoleon? Aulard asks whether, after the establishment of the consulate for life, leaving "nothing of the Republic but the name," there were those who wished to re-establish a true republic and whether there was still a republican party. He answers these questions by stating that among the most conspicuous democrats of 1794, Jeanbon Saint-André and Barère were the only ones to accept office in the new government, and "others, Robert Lindet, the two Prieurs, Cambon, Vadier, the former ministers Pache and Bouchotte, stood aloof." He then speaks of the republican opposition which included Carnot, Grégoire, Lanjuinais, Constant, and Chénier.[22] Lindet, during these years ardently wished for peace. He particularly deplored the Spanish and Russian adventures. On Napoleon's return from Elba he was approached to join the government, but refused. He claimed that his signature to the *Acte Additionnel* had been forged. This matter was to come up again after the Hundred Days.

In his retirement from public life, Lindet philosophized occasionally. On January 18, 1808, he wrote: "There is no religion or government that can resist time: it changes or modifies them from century to century. The Catholic religion and the monarchy

20. *Ibid.*, p. 384.
21. Palmer, *Twelve Who Ruled, op. cit.*, p. 392.
22. Aulard, *Histoire Politique, op. cit.*, p. 760.

existed in France for centuries. Only eternal providence is above these mutations and revolutions. In the midst of these upheavals, the human species preserves the principles of reason, of wisdom and virtue, which seemed effaced many times or entirely obscured, but which reappear in time . . . Preserve wisdom, justice, the virtues, be faithful to this eternal providence, avoid every kind of discouragement that increases misfortune—herein lies the duty of man. Hope speeds the return of happy days." At another time he wrote: "No man is more convinced than I that there has always been a religion on earth and that it is necessary that this be so. Any kind of religion is better than the absence of all religion." Montier remarks that the "lofty principles of deism guided his private conduct in a path of rigorous and wholesome austerity."[23]

During the Restoration, in 1816, official inquiries were made of the Lindet brothers.[24] The Under-Prefect at Bernay reported to the Prefect at Evreux on January 22, 1816, on Thomas Lindet, summarizing his life, and quoting Thomas' statement that he had held no office during the "usurpation of Bonaparte," and had not signed the *Acte Additionnel*. "He is now seventy-two and has always led an extremely retiring life both before and after the return of the usurper. He visits no one, this is incontestable, but . . . his home has always been a rendezvous of suspected persons."

The Under-Prefect then disposed briefly of Robert Lindet, who, he reported, "left Bernay for the Convention and since then has remained in Paris and has never returned to Bernay. He is richer than his brother through a marriage that he made with a Mlle. Mesnil . . . It is said that he is a consulting lawyer in Paris . . . It is not known whether or not he signed the *Acte Additionnel*." Correspondence from the office of General Police in Paris to the Prefect of the Eure on February 22, 1816, stated that investigation indicated that Robert Lindet had signed the *Acte Additionnel* and that further research would likely reveal that Thomas had also done so. The Prefect replied on February 26 that Thomas Lindet had not given his signature. Thomas addressed the mayor of Bernay on March 4, defending his own conduct, but taking even more

23. Montier, *op. cit.*, pp. 399–401.
24. Arch. Dep't. Eure 8m8. Enquête en Thomas et Robert Lindet en 1816, Bernay, 22 Janvier, 1816.

time to appeal most forcefully that the suspicions against his brother—in danger of being exiled—be removed.

The Law of Amnesty of January 12, 1816, in Article 7, excluded those regicides who had signed the *Acte Additionnel* or who had accepted employment under Napoleon during the Hundred Days. Robert Lindet, one of the 206 surviving regicides, sent to Barbé-Marbois, the Minister of Justice, a defense of those of his former associates who risked falling under the terms of the law. This un-dated document was registered on January 8, when the law was being debated in the Chamber of Peers.[25] Jean Vidalene remarks that "Robert Lindet, by this courageous measure, called attention to his existence. He maintained that he had not signed the *Acte Additionnel* and thus did not fall under the provisions of the law." The General Police, however, reported that he had signed the *Acte* on February 22, rather than on the 20th as had been first alleged. The police claimed that his signature had been verified by experts. Lindet was permitted, however, to remain in France because of poor health. Vidalene comments that, since Lindet's health was not as bad as that of others who were exiled, even after careful examination, the government must have had doubts of either the integrity or the competence of the handwriting experts.

Lindet, in his communication to the Minister of Justice, quoted the *Charte Constitutionnel*, Article II, that read: " 'All investigations of opinions and votes before the Restoration are forbidden; the same oblivion is ordered for the courts and for citizens.' " He commented that "This is the simplest, clearest, and most absolute statement in the Charter" and that the Charter and the spirit of Article II had been well accepted by all the Powers. "There are no longer regicides in France . . . There are only faithful subjects, devoted to the King, the monarchy, to the *Charte Constitutionnel* . . . One is never to recall the memories of terrible events. The past should be effaced from memory. The latest calamities to afflict France . . . [the Hundred Days] made us look

25. Arch. Nat'l. BB 30, 191–3, introduced and quoted by J. Vidalene, "Un plaidoyer de Robert Lindet en faveur des régicides en 1816," *Annales Historiques de la Révolution Française*, No. 102, Avril-Juin, 1945, pp. 156–161.

forward to an amnesty. This was the wish of all Frenchmen. An amnesty was announced. At once voices were raised demanding proscriptions . . . Had those who suggested this frightful charge read the *Charte*? . . . The *Charte* commanded forgetfulness . . . If the charges prevail the *Charte* is destroyed, the will of the King is defeated, the hope of the nations is frustrated, and tranquillity and security are subverted."

Lindet contended that the signatures of many to the *Acte Additionnel* were made under the duress of invasion and the promises of Napoleon to temper the rigors of his rule. "What did the signatures inscribed in the register signify? They attest to the fact that the weight of the dictatorship was insupportable. One treated this power with the appearance of submission and resignation that one must before all conquering force . . . The signatures of those in question . . . were only made through the prudence and practice permitted and authorized in every successful invasion; to declare these persons criminals, to proscribe them, means that opinions and votes prior to the Restoration are remembered. Thus the *Charte* will be annulled and the royal power will become powerless and vanquished . . . It is up to your Excellence to show the King that there are no regicides, scoundrels in France, that all men are faithful and devoted to his Majesty . . . I am with the most profound respect, Monseigneur . . . the very humble, very obedient servant. Lindet (*ancien avocat*)."

It is difficult to reconcile these expressions of fidelity to the monarchy with Lindet's unswerving republicanism unless it be that the ailing seventy-year old regicide so abhorred the Napoleonic aberration that he was willing to tolerate, hopefully, a constitutional monarchy. It is unlikely that it was opportunism, prompted by personal fear, that accounts for this communication.

Life was running out for the Lindet brothers. Thomas died on August 10, 1823, at eighty. The Church forbade a religious burial. Many followed the body to the unhallowed grave on August 11. There a speech was delivered which the Under-Prefect reported to his Prefect as being innocuous from the political point of view, "containing nothing reprehensible; [the speaker] spoke only of the beneficence and the spirit of M. Lindet, with no allusion, direct or indirect, contrary to the respect due to the Government."[26] Amand Montier says of the deceased: "He personified the spirit and aspirations of those Christian philosophers who, at the opening of the Revolution, had the generosity, or rather, the naivete, to believe in the disinterestedness of the privileged classes before the unanimous manifestation of the voice of the nation."[27]

Robert died two years later, on February 16, 1825, at seventynine and was buried in Père Lachaise cemetery.

How shall this modest and relatively unheralded revolutionary finally be evaluated? Etienne Charavay speaks most glowingly of him: "These three men [Carnot, Prieur de la Côte d'Or, and Lindet] were the incarnation of the very genius of the *patrie* and it is to their incessant collaboration that France owes her safety . . . With a sagacious and prudent mind, a calm and reflective nature, Robert Lindet did not yield to the caprice of opinion and to the violence of the passions; he resolved matters by the principles of sound reason . . . This man, so upright, so industrious, so humane, this incorruptible republican, this great citizen is one of the purest glories of the French Revolution."[28]

What Georges Bouchard said of Prieur (de la Côte d'Or) might well be said of Lindet: "Prieur was one of those men whom circumstances raised for a time above themselves."[29] There were in these men in the stirring and tumultuous days of the revolutionary convulsion, qualities of character and purpose, and disciplines of training that made them the instruments of a course hitherto unperceived or premeditated by them. They are to be measured as the frail and fallible men that most men are, who either failed or succeeded in fulfilling a significant role for good or ill in the cauldron of revolutionary upheaval.

Robert Lindet and his brother Thomas were representative of the considerable number of self-respecting, well-educated and ambitious professional men from the moderately prosperous provincial bourgeoisie, steeped in the ideas of the *philosophes*, who,

26. Arch. Dep't. Eure 9m7, Bernay, le 17 Aout 1823.
27. Montier, *Correspondance de Thomas Lindet, op cit.*, p. xiii.
28. Montier, *Robert Lindet, op. cit.*, Preface.
29. Bouchard, *Prieur, op. cit.*, p. 432.

with humane social impulses mixed with self-interest, were ready and willing to see the restrictive bonds of the Old Regime broken and a new society constructed.

In the life and career of Robert Lindet and of his less well-known brother, there is a consistent pattern of thought, conviction and action. There are some ambiguities, inconsistencies and contradictions in the conduct and speeches of Robert, particularly during the crises in the Revolution and in the persecutions of the regicides, especially those active in the government of the Terror, that followed 9 Thermidor and the Restoration. Despite these, Robert Lindet's life is essentially of one piece. He was not a man of clubs or factions; he abhorred extremism and violence, and steadily advocated harmony and reconciliation among the patriots. In him, at best, there is a balance of toleration, reasonableness, and the practical on the one hand, and the burning zeal of republicanism, with its faith in men, on the other.

Lindet's services to France in 1793–1795 are a matter of indisputable record. They have been factually narrated in these pages. With previous experience only at the local level, but with genuine administrative talents, he measured up effectively to the heavy tasks that were his in the national government. Recorded here is his staunch and unswerving devotion to republican principles and institutions. He was not one of the dynamic, colorful, or controversial figures in the Revolution. He was a bureaucrat *par excellence*, worked best alone, and had few intimates. His relationships with his brother were close and affectionate. In late middle age he demonstrated warm romantic feelings. On many occasions he proved to be a man of courage. At critical times he displayed unsolicited loyalty to his associates. That he loved his *patrie* is beyond dispute.

It may be that Robert Lindet rose above himself in the most critical days of the Revolution. To have lived through the Revolution, the Napoleonic Era, and into the Restoration without serious compromise attests to the character of the man.

Index

169